MORE PRAI[illegible]
Raising Great Parents

"*Raising Great Parents* is sure to bring out the best in both parents and children. It helps parents exit from frustrating and harmful power struggles with their kids and enter the realm of love, respect, and co-operation. This book offers a wise map for the parenting journey."

–*SARAH CHANA RADCLIFFE*, author of *Raise Your Kids Without Raising Your Voice* and *The Fear Factor*

"A giant step beyond reward and punishment, this book's focus on goal-oriented parenting offers hundreds of specific techniques designed to strengthen, rather than diminish, the formation of qualities that parents need so children can develop their full potential. The authors provide a gift of knowledge developed in three lifetimes of work with parents and children."

–*DR. FRANK WALTON*, Psychologist, Columbia, South Carolina, and Faculty Member, International Adlerian Summer Institute

"The program behind this book made more of a difference than I ever could have imagined. The principles are so logical, and my husband and our kids are enthusiastic supporters, too."

–*KATHLEEN TAYLOR*, Former President and CEO, Four Seasons Hotels and Resorts

"This book is current with neuroscience, educational theory, leadership principles, positive psychology, and systems thinking and is based on the best of what all of us have always wanted for our children. My own life was transformed when I first found out about how to apply these principles, and this book is a great way to learn and practice them. I love the idea that parents are working themselves out of their job – learning to 'unparent.'"

–***LINDA J. PAGE***, Ph.D., President of Adler School of Professional Studies and co-author of *Coaching with the Brain in Mind: Foundations for Practice*

Doone Estey
Beverley Cathcart-Ross
Martin Nash, M.D.

Raising Great Parents

How to Become the Parent Your Child Needs You to Be

Toronto & New York

Published in 2014 by
BPS Books
Toronto and New York
www.bpsbooks.com
A division of Bastian Publishing Services Ltd.

ISBN 978-1-927483-72-5 (paperback)
ISBN 978-1-927483-73-2 (ePDF)
ISBN 978-1-927483-74-9 (ePUB)

Cataloguing-in-Publication Data available from Library and Archives Canada.

Cover: Gnibel
Text design and typesetting: Casey Hooper

To all parents who seek to bring out the best in their children, their families, and themselves

Contents

Introduction

The journey that led us to write this book began in each of our homes, with our children. We started out like most parents we know. We wanted the best for our children; we wanted to protect them from making mistakes. As a result, we managed and controlled many details of their lives. We thought that because we knew better, they should listen to us every time their hair was messy, their homework was sloppy, or they left the house minus their coats.

Our kids, however, didn't appreciate our advice. They balked. Their message was clear: *You're not the boss of me! You can't make me!* They were right. We couldn't make them get out of the bath, eat their spaghetti, or even turn off the screen, especially if they were hiding it under the covers at bedtime. We couldn't force them to do anything, and they knew it.

FROM POWER STRUGGLE TO COOPERATION

Matters turned into a power struggle at home, and, as parents, we were frustrated. We thought that we and our families deserved better. Then we discovered a way out. We realized that, to end the stressful conflicts with our kids, we had to start with ourselves. We adopted a different form of parental leadership as it finally dawned on us that our challenge was not to raise great kids but to become great parents. We learned how rare are the children who do not respond well when the adults in their lives take the time to understand what they really want and need. We learned how to encourage our children's cooperation, respect their choices, and believe that they could manage the outcome. We dropped the command-and-control approach and started working with our children as a team.

Some of the key concepts in this book come from family doctor and psychotherapist Dr. Martin Nash, who has been counseling in Toronto for more than thirty-five years. When his first son turned three and became defiant, Martin didn't know what to do. Medical school hadn't trained him to handle the situation, so he and his wife, Georgine, turned to a 1966 book by American psychiatrist and educator Dr. Rudolf Dreikurs, *Children: The Challenge.* The new ideas they found there changed their life. They realized that children are smarter than we give them credit for; that there are underlying reasons for their behavior; that their actions are confirmations of their personal interpretation of the world.

As they probed Dreikurs' thinking, the Nashes understood something profound about kids: Love is not enough – children need respect for their own ideas and spirit. This, they realized, required a change in the role of the parent. *The job of a parent wasn't just to govern children but to teach them how to deal with life.* The job of parents was to work themselves out of a job.

Martin and Georgine began running study groups for parents who were having trouble with their children. One of those parents was Beverley Cathcart-Ross, and when she saw the impact of these ideas on her children and family, she became passionate about educating parents herself. She pursued the training required, launched Parenting Network in 1989, and created a highly successful series of courses for parents.

In the meantime, Doone Estey had been raising her children and training in parent education in the United States. When she returned to Toronto and completed her Adlerian training, she began running her own parenting courses and became equally dedicated to helping parents.

When Doone and Beverley crossed paths, they decided to join forces, and a new partnership began. As mothers and parent educators, we have expanded Parenting Network to include parenting courses in person, on CDs, on the telephone, and online. We have taken our workshops into schools and to parents in the workplace. For twenty-five years, we have taught tens of thousands of parents how to reduce their stress and inject joy into family life. We have learned from the parents in our classes. They shared their experiences and skills, and helped us develop the tools that form the basis of this book.

A NEW KIND OF LEADERSHIP

Raising Great Parents is about a new kind of leadership in the home. We're not talking about the top-down leadership model that was the norm a few decades ago. Instead, the leadership we describe here is based on collaboration. We give our children choices appropriate for their age and let them experience the outcome of those choices, provided that the situations are not life-threatening or hurtful to others.

It's wonderful to see how children respond to these opportunities. As they gain confidence and responsibility for their lives, they're far more willing to collaborate in and contribute to the home. They're more fun to be with. As are their parents! Best of all, when parents and children are on the same team, parents get closer to their kids. Take away the advice and orders, and kids tend to open up.

This doesn't mean we give in to their demands. This is a real problem for many of us parents today. We start out trying to guide our kids and then give up and give in to them. The kids end up ruling the roost, managing and controlling others – including us, their parents. No matter how we feel about it, this pushover parenting style is potentially bad for our children. They may grow up feeling entitled to the favored treatment they received at home and may not learn to respect the needs and wishes of others.

It is still the duty of parents to explain their point of view, draw the line between right and wrong, and prevent their kids from doing dangerous things. And there will be times when we'll determine that the situation requires our judgment to prevail. But most of the time, experience is a great teacher. Children need parents to provide them with a foundation of unconditional love and respect. They need parents to believe in them, no matter what. They need parents to guide them toward independence, responsibility, and self-confidence. To let go and give them opportunities to explore, to make decisions, to use their innate creativity ... even to struggle. When children see that they can handle the challenges of day-to-day life, and thus learn to believe in themselves, they grow stronger and more resilient. It's an exciting and rewarding process for all.

Our approach has helped thousands of parents enjoy the marvelous process of watching their children grow into great young people. Our hope is that, no matter where you are in your parenting journey, this book will become your go-to resource as you take on one of life's greatest challenges, becoming a great parent.

Before we begin, a word about you. If you're like most parents, you can be pretty hard on yourself by focusing on your mistakes and failures and by not appreciating your successes. That's why we like to practice CAW – Celebrate All Wins. We encourage you to congratulate yourself even for the smallest of wins, whether disengaging calmly from a defiant child instead of locking horns, going one hour without raising your voice, or getting out the door in the morning without a meltdown. There will always be another chance tomorrow.

A Note About the Exercises in This Book

Our goal from the beginning of our work has been to help parents shake up their parenting and get the results they want in their family life.

So, we thought, why not a book that replicates, as closely as possible, what parents experience in our parenting classes? A how-to book with ways to practice new skills throughout? A practical book full of examples and effective dialogue so that parents know what to say to their kids and why? Hence the exercises that you will find at the conclusion of each chapter, as well as the parenting pre- and post-quizzes at the beginning and end of the book.

We have seen how activities and examples make the difference between mediocre change and significant change. The parents we teach tell us that practice is what brings the ideas to life and that, hands down, it's much better than just reading in isolation or listening to a lecture. They love that we give them the words and preparation they need to avoid those meltdowns and invite their children to greater cooperation and closeness instead.

So, we have chosen the best from our classes, as well as some new inspirations, to share with you. We offer this book as a workbook – a platform on which you can build your parenting skills. It can become your own private journal or a way to discuss issues with your partner or a friend. By writing and talking about the examples you will learn more deeply. You'll then be ready with the tools in hand and the words on the tip of your tongue the next time you're faced with a parenting challenge – or, better said, opportunity.

Your Parenting Approach: A Pre-Quiz

The following will help you take stock of your current parenting approach. Please answer each question as honestly as possible. At the end of the book, you will have a chance to take stock again. We like to think of these quizzes as your parenting makeover, with a "before" and "after." You will see the progress you have made and the new skills you have learned. You will feel great about your parenting!

AS A PARENT, I ...	YOUR PRE-QUIZ RATING
Have fun, positive times with my child(ren)	No Sometimes Often Usually
Have a lot of worry and fear when it comes to parenting	No Sometimes Often Usually
Give my child(ren) a voice and say in decisions	No Sometimes Often Usually

Raise my voice or yell to be heard	No	Sometimes	Often	Usually
Have provided my child(ren) with regular jobs to do in the home	No	Sometimes	Often	Usually
Argue with my child(ren)	No	Sometimes	Often	Usually
Am comfortable with my child(ren) making mistakes or struggling	No	Sometimes	Often	Usually
Understand the reasons behind a child's misbehavior	No	Sometimes	Often	Usually
Use bribery, use threats, or remove privileges when my child(ren) don't cooperate	No	Sometimes	Often	Usually
Take time outs for myself until I calm down	No	Sometimes	Often	Usually
Use consequences to discipline my child(ren)	No	Sometimes	Often	Usually
Love my child(ren), no matter how they behave	No	Sometimes	Often	Usually
Apologize to my child(ren) when I make a mistake	No	Sometimes	Often	Usually
Have worked out morning and bedtime routines with my child(ren)	No	Sometimes	Often	Usually

See my child(ren) as able to handle their daily life	No	Sometimes	Often	Usually
Look for ways to improve life skills that my child(ren) will need for their future	No	Sometimes	Often	Usually
Am on the same parenting page as my partner	No	Sometimes	Often	Usually

Create the Right Atmosphere: Parenting for the Long Term

"Come on, honey, it's time to get up!"

"What have you been doing in here?"

"I don't want to ask you one more time!"

"I need you to get downstairs, or you'll be late for school!"

And that's just how the day *starts* for many parents. Then, when our child comes home, we cajole, nag, or issue more orders, sometimes at the top of our voices. This continues from the moment our child walks or slouches through the door until the time when he or she finally, reluctantly, turns out the light.

Sound familiar? Let's step outside this scene for a moment.

IMAGINING YOUR CHILD IN THE FUTURE

Imagine the day that your child enters those crucial teenage years. He or she turns sixteen. What do you hope he or she will be like? How would you like your friends and family to describe your child? What words do you think they'll use?

We ask these questions every time we start a new parenting class, and the words the parents suggest are nearly always the same: Confident. Self-motivated. Independent. Caring. Empathetic. Optimistic. Responsible. Respectful. Honest. Curious. Wise. Resilient.

Try this thought experiment yourself. Better still, write the words down. You might want your kids to be independent in their thinking and show good judgment to help guard against extreme risk-taking behaviors. You might want them to be responsible for their stuff and their commitments and their deadlines. Maybe you pick empathy, kindness, and community-mindedness as priorities.

It is significant that the characteristics parents instinctively list are the very qualities children will need to develop to their full potential both personally and professionally.

But guess what? There's one word parents never suggest: Obedient. That might be a valuable attribute for children who end up working in an organization where the credo is "do what you're told"; however, most of the time, obedience is not going to make a person happy or successful. Truth be told, it is not a trait that pops into our minds when we imagine our children in the future.

GOAL-ORIENTED PARENTING

To parent for the long term is to parent with goals in mind. And the goal-oriented approach doesn't apply only to the wishes we have for our children. It applies to us, as parents. Think about your relationship with your children: What are your goals? Would you like to stop raising your voice? Be more confident in your decision making? Would you like to be less fearful when the kids walk out the door? Would you like to feel better in your everyday interactions with your kids? To stop threatening or bribing or punishing? To put the joy back into parenting? That last one alone is a valuable goal.

The choices we make every day will affect how our children experience their early developing years. Will they remember a childhood full of warmth and fun and closeness with the people they love the most? Or will they remember the battles with parents and siblings, or have that feeling of distance that these struggles and conflicts can generate? Scientists have found that a significant part of behavior is genetic, but the rest comes from experience and choices – from the world we live in. That world, for our children, begins with us and the home life we build.

We have big, long-term goals for our children. The question now is this: What are we doing right now, on a day-to-day basis, to realize them? What are we saying to our children, in word and gesture and action, throughout the day? In our courses, we find most parents say things like the following to their children:

"Jas, you're taking too long in there. How many times do I have to tell you we've got to go?"
"I am not going to ask you again. You need to sit down and practice the piano."
"Hurry up! Are you listening to me?"

"Just go to bed. I'll deal with this tomorrow."

What are we doing here? Are we parenting to help our children achieve the long-term goals we just listed, or are we parenting just to get through the day? Are we being the parents we want to be, or are we turning into the crazy persons we swore we would never become? We need to get our children out the door in the morning in time for school so we can go to our jobs or deal with our to-do list. So we end up parenting by the moment, and not necessarily by a method that we are proud of. We just react to whatever the children throw at us and throw our long-term goals out the window at the same time.

ADDRESSING A FUNDAMENTAL CONTRADICTION IN PARENTING

To make matters worse, our kids have the same long-term goals that we do: independence, self-control, responsibility, respect, and self-motivation.

Their perspective, however, is different. Their timing, their priorities, and their values do not always coincide with ours. This is why, when we ask our children to listen, to cooperate, or to do as we say, they often don't. Obedience is the furthest thing from their minds.

How do we address the fundamental tension between our short-term and long-term parenting goals? How can we stop working against ourselves and our children? The answers are in this book.

MAGIC BULLET
The Short and Long of It

Many parents find themselves getting caught up in short-term parenting. In so doing, they neglect to equip their children with the resilience, independence, and confidence they need to handle the ups and downs of life. Children need to learn many life skills in order to become high-functioning adults. One of the primary responsibilities of parents is to encourage these life skills from the time their children are toddlers.

We need to stop being reactive and adopt a more reflective and reasoned approach. When our children are not in a life-threatening situation, which is most of the time, we can take the time to assess the situation. Then we can decide what we can do and say that will help our child meet the needs of the situation – getting to bed on time, for example. We can take a proactive approach instead of a reactive one. If we're trying to teach the life skills and qualities that we value so highly, we're better off using words and gestures that will encourage them, not undermine them.

We need to parent with one eye always on our long-term goals. If the goal is for our children to be responsible for themselves, for example, why do we remind them all the time to do their homework, remember their lunchbox, and brush their teeth? Does it make any sense to do all of this for them and protect them from possible mistakes? If we want our children to be independent thinkers, does it make any sense to tell them what to do, even if we're offering well-meaning advice? If we want our children to respect themselves and others, does it make any sense to yell at them? Won't they just learn from us and start yelling, too?

Parenting for long-term goals can sometimes look odd or even counterintuitive in the short term. Say your eight-year-old son dawdles, complains about what's for dinner, and wants you to do everything. If you're like most, you might react, get angry, and either snap or show your disapproval so you can get him to bed on time. You might even feel a little resentful as you do it. Parenting in this manner on a daily basis is inconsistent with – and even antithetical to – your long-term goals for your children and for yourself as a parent.

This book demonstrates how you can reconcile this contradiction. We propose a solution that combines achieving your long-term goals for your children with a day-to-day approach to all your parenting challenges. What we suggest is this: Instead of yelling over spilled orange juice in the kitchen, reconsider for a moment and be proactive in your next actions. Take a deep breath, and then recruit your child to help solve the problem and possibly clean it up. You will be encouraging your child to take another step toward independence, responsibility, and respectfulness.

Our kids need to learn and believe that they can handle both successes and failures. They have to have opportunities to be independent, curious, and responsible. They need chances to discover their strengths and weaknesses and learn how to build on them. Children need to know that they are valued no matter how things turn out. Their feelings and self-esteem shouldn't go up and down like a yo-yo with every misstep or failure.

We believe it is possible to parent with long-term goals firmly in mind *and* get through the day. This may be hard to believe when your children are supposed to be brushing their teeth but instead are fighting over who gets to squeeze the toothpaste, when eating dinner degenerates into finger painting with their food, or when they want to wear their pajamas to dinner but not to bed. It's hard to imagine that you can parent in a logical way, with long-term goals in mind, when you're dealing with a child who knows exactly how to push your buttons and drive you crazy.

But you can. So let's begin!

EXERCISE: LONG-TERM GOALS FOR YOUR CHILDREN

1. List your long-term goals for your children.

2. Beside the list, place a column for each of your children. On a scale of 1 to 10, indicate how your child is doing against each of these goals. These scores will indicate where your child has strengths and weaknesses *at this point in time.*

3. Reflect on what you may be doing right now to encourage or possibly discourage the development of these skills. Write this down.

4. Every few weeks, look for signs that they are progressing toward the goals. Revisit the number you indicated above for their progress and revise, as necessary.

EXERCISE: SHORT-TERM GOALS FOR YOURSELF

1. Think about your strengths as a parent. Write down three of them.

    1.

    2.

    3.

2. Now look at your challenges as a parent: Perhaps you want to stop yelling or stop repeating yourself. You may want to deal more effectively with your child when he or she dawdles in the morning. These are all fine goals. Write down three of them for yourself.

    1.

    2.

    3.

3. Each week, track the progress you make on your goals, on a scale of 1 to 10. You can ask your children for their views!

Your Attitude Makeover: Parenting with Love, Respect, and Belief

Our approach to parenting is based on LRB – unconditional ***love*** and approval for the child (not necessarily for their behavior), ***respect*** for the child's right to make some decisions and choices, and ***belief*** in the child's ability to handle the outcome of these choices. Children need all three of these from parents in order to be secure and strong and to have the self-confidence to deal with whatever life presents.

LOVE

They love me, they love me not ...

We all love our children. But if we take a look at what we actually say and do, what are we showing them? What message are we giving to our children in the words we choose, the behaviors we display, and the tone of our voice?

Is it: *I love you just as you are*? Or is it: *I love you only if you listen, if you behave yourself, if you turn off the TV*?

Now, we all know our love for our children is unconditional. We love them no matter what. Who would ever say, "I love my child only if she cleans up her room?" No one! Yet what we say and do can send a message we do not intend.

Throughout the day, we may find ourselves saying:

"I will be upset with you if ..."
"I will be disappointed in you if ..."
"It would make me happy if you ..."

WHAT A YOUNG CHILD WANTS

It's interesting to consider how children interpret our words. From the child's point of view, it doesn't matter what we intend. She'll interpret our words and especially the emotional message of our delivery from her point of view. What a young child wants is very simple: our love and approval. If we show, with our words and emotions, that we are angry or upset with our child over a certain behavior, she will interpret it like this:

"Mom or Dad will love me more, or less, if I behave a certain way."

She will think that we love her more if she performs as we wish, and less if she trips up. She'll think that our love is conditional, and this may affect her the rest of her life.

We may think that she has misinterpreted us, but has she?

We may also be sending the message that our happiness depends on her behavior. Could we be trying to guilt her or bribe her into doing something so we can feel better about our parenting? This situation is all too common.

For example, our son does something noteworthy at school or at home, and we practically beam our love at him. But then, when he isn't doing his homework and he's ignoring our nagging reminders, we furrow our brow, sigh with frustration, and allow an edge to enter our voice. Or we snap. So our child may think, *Mom or Dad doesn't love me right now.* When a child believes this, it hurts – and it can feed a feeling of insecurity that will be highly detrimental over time.

Losing a parent's love and approval hurts a child more than anything, and it will cause one of three reactions. The child:

- Hurts back in retaliation
- Tries to win our love back by being obedient or pleasing
- Gives up and retreats into his shell

Whichever way, the child is discouraged and feels insecure.

WHAT HAPPENED TO OUR UNCONDITIONAL LOVE?

Why do we parents say things that make it sound as if our love for our children is conditional? We don't start out this way. We give our newborn infants unconditional love so freely, even when they cry all night. We think they're little miracles, so full of hope and promise. But in no time we're facing a ten-month-old baby who arches her back when it's time for her diaper to be changed. We find ourselves saying things like, "I'll be unhappy with you if don't lie still." We can be sure the baby gets the message.

Many parents say these things because they think it will motivate their child to perform cooperatively and successfully. They believe their children will behave appropriately only if they are prodded or threatened. Now, it's true that this approach may achieve what we might want in the moment, but at what cost? It can set up some pushback from our child or make dependence on us their motivator, but it certainly won't promote closeness or relational harmony.

The biggest price, though, is paid by the child. If parents appear happy or sad as a result of a child's performance, the child not only sees this judgment but also internalizes good or bad feelings about himself, based on his parents' approval or disapproval.

The child begins to take it as a given that *How well I perform = How much I am loved.* Even when our intent as parents is to motivate our kids to win and not lose, to be a success and not a failure, the cost is high. Our children may feel that they're never good enough. Even 90 percent on an exam is not good enough. Winning the soccer game is good this week, but now the pressure to win next week becomes even higher. Children brought up in this climate of performance anxiety may feel frightened and tense, with fleeting pulses of joy when they win.

OUR SOLUTION

The solution to this dilemma is simple: Accept your children as they are. Give them unconditional love. They need to know that, no matter how they perform, they can count on your unconditional love and support. An atmosphere of unconditional love will enable your children to develop a strong sense of belonging and security.

How do you do this in practice? We think the best advice comes from the great American psychiatrist and educator Rudolf Dreikurs. He says:

- Separate the deed from the doer.
- Make it perfectly clear: *I love you, not necessarily your behavior.*

If, for instance, your child is yelling at you, you could say: "I care about what you have to say; however, I'm not willing to be yelled at." What we're really saying is that we won't always love everything our child does, but our love for her is never in question. Or, say your child is not getting ready for school in the morning. You could try telling her: "Clara, it's frustrating how long you're taking to get ready for school today. What can we do about this?"

Even if you find yourself raising your voice more than you wish, you can make sure she knows that you're addressing her behavior, not her.

We recommend that you build unconditional love into every day with your kids. An easy way to get started with this is to adopt the ritual that we call Three Greetings with Hugs. Hugging is fundamental to this ritual because it is a physical demonstration of the love we declare.

- The first greeting in a child's day is, of course, in the morning. We suggest that, instead of "Come on, get out of bed, we don't want to be late," you try something warm and caring, for example, "It's great to see you! I need one of your hugs. Last night's has all worn off." Share the unbridled joy you have for your children. Then you can focus on the needs of the morning. Get that greeting and close connection with them in there first. They may say, "Go away," and pull the covers over their heads, but that's okay. The message got through.
- The second greeting and hug is when you reunite – when you pick them up at school or get home from work. Before anything else, let your kids know they're the most important person in that moment. A hug, a warm greeting, or a few words about how we thought about them during that day does the trick. They might hit us with their lunch box and say, "You make yucky lunches," but we know our words of unconditional love got in there, and they learn, yet again, that they don't have to do anything to earn our love. It has nothing to do with their performance – it's there no matter what.
- The third important greeting in the day is bedtime. Even if things went off the rails and got ugly during the day, it's great to send them into the land of nod with assurances of our love, in word and action.

Of course you can share your love more frequently than this, but this practice provides a powerful daily baseline of love and acceptance.

Showing affection can be easier for some parents than others. But even if you have trouble with it, this is a good time to dig deep. Research has indicated over and over again the power of closeness. It's good for all children, even your teenager. Affection can be as simple as a big smile, a loving rub of their shoulder, or a wink from across the room. Or you might pull them up onto your lap for a cuddle, or have a wrestle on the floor.

Bottom line: Love is not supposed to be a tool to manipulate our children's behavior. It should not be used as a reward or a punishment. When we shower our children with unconditional love, it provides them with a secure and safe place to use their internal creativity to grow, learn, and flourish.

RESPECT

What does respect mean? We define it a little differently than you might expect. Most of us are looking for mutual respect in relationships: *I respect you and you respect me.* While this is ideal, it has a flaw. You can respect someone, but you cannot control whether that person respects you back. You can respect your child, but you cannot force your child to respect you. So we advocate what we call Dual Respect: being respectful of others, including your children, and at the same time being respectful of yourself.

Let's talk about respect for children first. Every child is born with a strong, natural desire to learn, explore, and be creative. We respect this. We want this to flourish. We don't want to stamp it out. This means we respect even a toddler's wonderful ability to learn. Therefore it's important that we give our children opportunities to make decisions and judgments for themselves (as long as the situation isn't harmful or destructive).

- A three-year-old can choose which cereal goes in her bowl.
- A six-year-old can decide what she wants to wear to school. Even if her clothing choice looks odd to our eyes, this is her choice.
- A twelve-year-old can manage his own homework schedule.

We don't have to agree with the judgment of our twelve-year-old or six-year-old. Lots of times we wouldn't make the choices they make. But when we show we respect their ability, as young human beings, to choose for themselves, our children can learn to manage many aspects of their daily lives and enjoy that great feeling of self-reliance and independence.

A POWERFUL PARENTAL ENDORSEMENT

When we respect our children's abilities to make a choice, we're not too concerned with the outcome. Many of their choices won't work out very well because they haven't developed their judgment yet. But we want them to gain the experience and confidence they need to make good choices. We feel that experience is the best teacher; it's much stronger than words. This attitude is a powerful endorsement from a parent.

Here's another way of looking at it. If you choose to play Father Knows Best and tell a child what to do, what you're really saying is: "I know better. I have more experience and knowledge, so you need to listen to me." On top of that the child may hear, "You're not smart enough to handle this." That message, intentional or not, really hurts. It makes a child feel incapable, and it may trigger retaliation. So the next time your child asks you what to do, consider turning it around: "What do you think would be best?" You could even ask for your child's help on a problem that *you* have.

As a parent, you need to respect yourself and remember that you have a choice. Some parents forget this part of the deal, perhaps because they're worried that if they draw the line, their child will rebel or withdraw. You don't have to do what your child says. When you are respectful of yourself, you can be the leader instead, saying clearly what you are willing to do and what you are not.

After all, there's only one person you can be absolutely sure of controlling, and that's you. So the next time your child talks back to you in a way you don't like, you have the option of creating some space for yourself by saying, or just thinking, something like this: "I respect you as a child, even if you aren't being respectful at the moment. I will respect myself. So I'm going to go to my room for a few minutes, and when I get back we'll try again."

MAGIC BULLET
Attitude

"Actions speak louder than words. But attitude speaks loudest of all!"

Attitude in parenting is key. So few parenting books address this vital part of a parent's communication. It's not just what we do, but how we do it.

Our attitude is an accumulation of our own childhood and life experiences, values, and beliefs. The medium for expressing our attitude is our tone of voice and body language.

Kids easily sense when the words coming out of our mouth don't match the message our tone and body are sending. They read our attitude and then make a decision and choose an action based on what they believe we are conveying. A four-year-old boy once said to his mom, "Let me look in your eyes. Are you angry in there?"

If your child is badgering you while you're on the phone, you might say, "I'm unable to hear the person on the phone. Can you be patient and wait until I'm finished, or do I need to take the call in another room?" If the behavior doesn't improve, you could go into another room to continue the call or carve out some quiet time for yourself. This is what respecting yourself looks like, and when you deliver the message in a kind tone of voice, you're also showing respect for your child. You're saying, in effect, "I can't make you do it, so I will decide for myself what I will do in this situation. I'm not willing to be treated disrespectfully, and I am going to decide what's going to happen next – to me, not to you."

PARENTING WITH SELF-RESPECT

Thinking about what you will do can be useful in many challenging situations. Consider a situation in which your child is arguing with you. You could say, "This isn't working for me. I need a break. When we're both calm, I'll be willing to hear what you want to tell me." You could even give yourself a time out and walk into your bedroom for some breathing space.

Or say your children are fighting at story time, and it's driving you crazy. There's an easy way for you to restore some balance for yourself – by tapping once again into this principle of self-respect. Here's how: You can close the book and say, "I will read when the room is quiet." Now you have control – over yourself.

In effect, your words mean, "I can't make you do it, so I will decide for myself what I will do in this situation. I'm going to behave with self-respect and decide what's going to happen next – to me."

DUAL RESPECT

Let's look further at this concept of Dual Respect.

No matter what the situation, ask yourself the question, "How do I show respect for my child and at the same time maintain my self-respect?"

TWO KINDS OF POWER AND CONTROL

- Power and control over others
- Power and control over ourselves

Unless you're in a life-threatening situation, exercising power over others is disrespectful and detrimental in any relationship. You have power and control only over yourself.

The goal in a cooperative, collaborative relationship is to offer your love, to offer your ideas, and to guide – not to dominate and control.

For example, your son has his heart set on a rather expensive pair of running shoes. You get annoyed because you don't have, or aren't willing to spend, the money they cost. You don't want him to succumb to peer pressure, either. He cries and carries on, telling you that everybody else has these shoes and that he'll be ostracized unless he has them, too.

You can understand his wish to be part of the "in crowd," but you've also got a limit on how much you'll spend on this kind of footwear. What can you do?

Lots of parents get stuck in this situation, but here's something that we find can work: Tell him that you're willing to contribute toward the cost of the shoes, and he can make up the shortfall from his own saved-up allowance or in lieu of a birthday or Christmas present.

If he objects, calmly and lovingly ask him if he has any other ideas to help solve this problem. You, however, will continue to show self-respect in your actions.

Children learn by watching their parents' behavior. When parents model respect for themselves in all of their relationships, their children learn to respect themselves and the people they love, too.

Our goal is to give you more confidence as a parent. We think parents should take on their role as family leaders and not let their children run the show. While we respect our children's desire to get their own way, we need to model respect for ourselves, too. Our role is to encourage our children to consider others and use their desire to explore and be creative in a more cooperative and collaborative way. It's Dual Respect, a win-win.

BELIEF

It's natural for us as parents to want to protect our children or offer advice to guide them and prevent them from making mistakes. Many of us feel we have to have the last word, and we keep talking to make sure we do. We remind, give warnings, and manage. So, when we go to the playground when they're five, we say:

"Don't climb that high, Johnny!"
"Watch your feet!"
"Be careful or you'll fall!"

Or, when they're twelve:

> *"You don't want to wear that to school. Everyone will tease you."*
> *"Where's your backpack? Have you got everything in it?"*
> *"Hurry up; you don't want to be late."*

They call us pillow parents. We're smothering our children. Or, to use another metaphor, we're bubble-wrapping them to protect them from life.

CONFIDENCE AND FAITH VS. FEAR

Why do we do this? Our primal instinct is to keep our kids safe and secure. We are parenting from fear, so we opt for the "tried and true," thinking this will give us a better chance of controlling the outcome. But what are we accomplishing here? Are we helping our children to be independent, to be confident in their decisions when exploring their world, to avoid taking foolish risks? Clearly not. Instead, we're sending them the clear message that they can't handle the challenges and risks of their world.

We need to believe that our children will handle the outcomes of their choices, whether they're successful or not. Yes, if they fall in the playground, they might get a few scrapes. They might make a mistake, or even fail. But the kids will be all right: Their scrapes will heal, and they will always have the opportunity to learn from their experiences. They'll develop resilience, the ability to bounce back, and they'll realize that they can cope with failure and mistakes. They'll also develop what we call copability – the ability to cope with the potholes of life and not stay hurt. Our children need these important characteristics to live a happy, healthy, and successful life.

This means that, as parents, we need to stand aside whenever possible and let our children experience the results of their choices. We can be a safety net when needed or a cheering team in the background. The key is to let our children see our confidence in their ability to manage what comes their way. This isn't easy, particularly when we think we know just how to prevent the problem or mistake. In fact, it's counterintuitive. Yet, if we step in to prevent a mistake, we'll erode our children's confidence in their own ability to handle their lives. Experience in handling the inevitable failures is the greatest teacher. It is actually what builds a child's self-confidence.

It takes time and practice to master this approach. To start, you might ask yourself if the thing your child is about to do is life-threatening. Most of the time it won't be. In that case, be confident that your child will survive, bounce back, and heal, even if she sheds a few tears along the way.

A MESSAGE OF BELIEF IN YOUR CHILD

Instead of offering your advice, no matter how good it may be, send the message, "You can handle it. Even if it doesn't work out the way you want, you'll learn from it, and it will help you do better next time."

If your four-year-old is having trouble tying her shoelaces, for instance, it may be tempting to do it for her because it's faster and easier that way. That may be so, but there's real value in

DEFINING "ENHANDLEMENT" AND FEAR

Enhandlement: To foster our children's self-confidence and desire to go ahead and explore, be creative, take risks, and not stay embarrassed or hurt when they make mistakes or their efforts aren't successful.

Fear: Anxiety, stress, and worry are different intensities of fear. These are all signals to us and can be viewed in a positive light. We should respect and appreciate our brain's radar capabilities. See the signal as a friend. The key is not to see it as a solution.

We like to use the word "enhandlement" rather than "encouragement." "Encouragement" conveys the default position of fear from which a child is expected to come up with the courage to overcome a situation or achieve success. "Enhandlement" conveys the default position of confidence and belief - that the child will be able to handle each situation.

And really, for all of us, most things in life don't require courage so much as a belief that we can handle what comes our way.

holding back and saying, "Go ahead, give it a try. You'll figure this out soon with a little practice," or, "Shoelaces can be tough! Your brain and fingers will work it out soon enough. So don't give up trying!" This gives your child an opportunity to learn for herself.

If your ten-year-old is doing his homework and asks you the meaning of a word, don't just give him the answer. You might say instead, "Why don't you check that out in the dictionary or on the computer?"

The message you want to convey is that you won't always be there to answer his questions, so it's important for him to learn to be independent and resourceful.

It's possible to be confident in your child and in yourself even when your child isn't cooperating. For example, your seven-year-old child is dawdling in the morning and not getting ready for school. It's hard not to snap, but it might help to think these positive and encouraging thoughts: *You are a lovable, creative, and able child. Right now there's a problem that needs our attention. Once we figure this out, I'm confident that you will behave more cooperatively. It may not turn out perfectly, but we'll both learn from this. This, too, will pass!*

THIS, TOO, WILL PASS

Parents in our courses love the statement, "This, too, will pass." It gives them the confidence they need to have some faith both in their child and themselves. Just thinking these words can help because they govern how we feel, what we say and do, and our body language.

Consider, for example, what happens when you think critical and discouraging thoughts: *You're always being difficult and selfish. Why can't you just listen for a change and cooperate? I give up, you drive me crazy.*

Read these words aloud and listen to your tone of voice.

If this is the story you tell yourself about your child, how do you think it will affect what you say and do? How will that affect your child's belief in his ability to handle things?

Showing confidence in a child's ability to handle life's challenges takes time, practice, and an encouraging attitude. But it's well worth the effort. When we believe in our children, they'll learn to believe in themselves. So make the investment now. Sprinkle some faith around them. Let them skin their knees. Let them experience and learn to handle the hurts in life. They'll be stronger for it, and your investment will provide untold returns, saving both you and your children lots of misery later on.

EXERCISE: TAKING CARE OF YOURSELF

"Put your oxygen mask on first before putting one on your child."

How many times have we heard this direction when we're about to take off in a plane? We never give it a second thought. The point is that we are useless to anyone else if we are not functioning properly ourselves.

It's a point worth remembering in our day-to-day lives as parents. All too often, we put our own needs on the back burner to meet what we perceive to be the needs of our children. But what children really need are well-rested, well-exercised, and well-cared-for parents. Not only do we function and feel better, but children learn to take care of themselves when they see us doing it.

We are role models for our children. They observe what we eat for breakfast, how often we brush our teeth, how much wine we drink, whether we are always rushed, how we manage conflict, and how we deal with our feelings. We must attend to some of our own needs, and we must let our kids see us doing it, so they, in turn, will learn to take care of themselves.

It's not just a question of paying attention to our physical and mental health, either. Practicing self-respect is just as important as watching our diet, exercise, and sleep patterns.

When the two of us were at home with our respective kids, it was pretty hard to carve out some time for ourselves. But we knew of many small ways in which we could practice self-respect. Not that it worked all the time, mind you, but that was the plan.

We'd say things like:

> *"No, I'm sorry, but story time is over. It's time for me to say goodnight."*
>
> *"I'm not willing to do any more puzzles. Mom is all puzzled out!"*
>
> *"Yes, we're having something I like for dinner for a change."*
>
> *"I'm going to take a bath now for twenty minutes ... by myself."*
>
> *"I'm not willing to argue with you. It's your night to do the dishes."*
>
> *"I will drive you to the mall when the den is clean."*
>
> *"I'm going to go to my room for a while to calm down and collect my thoughts."*

Think of two recent situations in which you interacted with your kids with less than a full tank of self-respect. Describe them here and include how you responded.

1.

2.

3.

Now write down some statements like the ones above that you will say the next time similar situations arise. Be sure to reflect your feeling of self-respect in your wording:

1.

2.

3.

Some of these approaches take patience and determination and require disengaging when our children decide to retaliate with some bad behavior. Children are persistent and can wear us down, but we can be careful not to give in to their demands.

Setting limits for ourselves is worth it in the long run as our children learn resilience, self-control, and what mom or dad's boundaries are. When we show self-respect and decide what we will or will not do, we also show our children what self-respect looks like in action. This knowledge will help them build self-confidence and healthy relationships.

List here three things you're going to do each day to "oxygenate" yourself with self-respect. You'll be happier as a result. So will your kids.

1.

2.

3.

"I Said Turn Off the TV": From Power Plays to Collaboration

It's time for dinner, and your ten-year-old, Susie, is zoned out in front of the TV. You say, in a pleasant but firm voice, "Would you please turn off the TV? It's time for dinner."

Susie keeps watching. Two minutes later, you say it again, this time with your sharper "don't test me, young lady" tone of voice: "Susie, I said turn off the TV!"

Two minutes later when you march into the room, the TV is still on. Smoke starts coming out your ears and you snap. The sergeant major voice takes over. "That's it. Turn it off now, or there will be no more TV until you're sixteen. Do you understand?" Pause. "Did you hear me?"

Could this be you some of the time, or even all of the time? It might be the TV, it might be bedtime, or it might be something simple, like getting your child dressed after a fun afternoon at the pool. But the pattern is the same: You think you're making a request, a sensible and reasonable request, and you say it nicely. But then your child does not comply, so you have to issue orders. What else can you do? You want the best for your child, and you feel you know better. If you don't order your child to turn off the TV, she'll end up watching all day. How else are you supposed to get that thing turned off?

This chapter looks at how we're operating right now as parents. We'll see that each of us uses a certain approach or style when we deal with our kids, and some of us might even use a few styles throughout the day. Which style is it? Well, it boils down to a choice between two main themes:

- *The struggle for power*: Who's on top? Who's getting his way? Do you have the power over your child, or does your child have the power over you? It becomes a competition.
- *Cooperation and collaboration*: How are you going to work together to meet the needs of the situation, and how is your child going to contribute to the family and in life?

THE STRUGGLE FOR POWER

WHEN A PARENT DOMINATES: THE CONTROLLING PARENT

This style of parenting is a modern version of the way most of our parents used to do it. A generation ago, many parents just told their kids what to do. They expected them to obey or else, which usually meant some form of physical punishment.

Today we want to do things a little differently. Instead of using physical punishment or force, we want to guide our children and show them the right way to do things, saving them the trouble of making mistakes and the pain of getting hurt. Instead of taking the superior position and issuing orders and expecting our children to submit out of fear or intimidation, we want to be reasonable and respectful when we ask our children to do things.

Like the parent asking her child to turn off the TV before dinner, we start out politely. But if our children don't accept our suggestions, we find we quickly revert to the role of the controlling parent – a controller wearing kid leather gloves, perhaps, but a controller all the same. This means we tell our children to "just do it!" and expect them to comply. We think we're behaving like a caring teacher offering experience and ideas. But if we expect the recipient of our advice to obey, we're no longer acting like teachers. We're in dictator mode.

Do you ever find yourself saying or thinking:

"It's funny how kids don't seem to listen these days."
"Somehow they just don't do what I tell them to do; I can hardly believe my eyes."
"I would have never gotten away with this when I was a kid, that's for sure."

The attitude behind these statements is what's behind the sharply worded orders we issue when being polite and asking nicely don't work. And if our orders don't work, we dig deeper into our arsenal of blame, threats, and punishments:

"What have you been doing up here? I told you we don't have time for play."
"The trouble with you is that you never listen!"
"If you are not ready by the time I count to three, there will be no story tonight!"
"It's your own fault. If you weren't so slow, you would have had time for breakfast."
"How many times have I asked you to get dressed? It's so easy – just get dressed."
"I am sick and tired of telling you kids to stop fighting. I can't believe you took his pencil – now give it back!"
"Don't take such big mouthfuls, don't gulp your food, don't talk with your mouth full."
"Hurry up!"
"I can't believe you haven't brushed your teeth. Do you want them all to fall out?"
"If you touch your brother one more time I am going to scream and no, I don't care that he touched you first."

This is not how we hoped to be as parents, yet here we are playing Judge, Cop, and Boss, handing out rewards and punishments, depending on external motivation. We set rules, and we react to our kids' behavior with approval or, more often, disapproval. Just think of how often we start sentences with the words *no* and *don't*.

The very real danger here is that we end up in a competition with our child. We believe we should get our way. After all, we know what's best. We believe we're right, so we feel our child

MAGIC BULLET
Benevolent Dictators

Most parents we meet don't want to yell or fight with their children at all. And they would not characterize themselves as dictators. However, we regularly hear the complaint from parents that their children just don't listen. "I ask them nicely three times to do something and then I snap!" We call this being a benevolent dictator.

Children are quick to clue in when a parent isn't making a request but is making a demand disguised as a request.

should listen to us. When our child does something good, we show our love. But if our child refuses to follow, we might use threats or a dose of fear to get our child to submit: "If you don't come now, I'm leaving the park without you!"

Many of us turn to this style of parenting because it is so familiar. But it also comes from a reflex we are born with to be superior, not inferior; to win, not lose. We naturally want our children to behave properly, to be on time, be responsible, be successful. We think we know how to achieve this, and we tell them. We want them to do what we say because it's safer that way, both physically and emotionally. *I'm telling you this for your own good*, we think. If they don't obey, our worry kicks in and fear for our children's future swamps us. *How will they turn out if they don't do things properly now? If she's acting like this at six, what will she do when she's sixteen?*

Yet what's the cost of this style of parenting? What's the impact of this controlling style on our children? Here's one way to find out. Ask yourself: What would it feel like to be on the receiving end of these orders? Imagine you are your child. You are being bossed around, controlled, and told to brush your teeth now, or else! How would you feel? What would you think?

In our classes, we ask some parents to stand on a chair and play the parent, and others to sit on the floor and play the child, looking up and listening to all the orders. It's amazing to watch the parents who are in the children's role. When they hear the string of orders, some roll their eyes. Others clearly are tuning out. Later, when we talk about it, we find that there is one thing they all agree on – the "parent" made them feel disrespected, shamed, humiliated, small, stupid, fearful, controlled, stifled. It's all hurtful. The majority say their reflex is to push back and be difficult or defiant. We rarely hear anyone say they felt like jumping to it and doing what they were told.

When a child's right to have a voice or say is stifled by a parent, the child is limited to two main options. One option is to submit and conform to please the parent out of fear of getting into trouble. This kind of child will tend to play it safe and shy away from using natural creativity to solve problems. It's too risky. The other option is to defy or retaliate. The child can do this overtly, by saying, in effect, "You're not the boss of me," or covertly, by dawdling or ignoring or becoming "parent deaf." Parents of children with this "hearing problem" often think their kids are living in another world, but make no mistake about it, they actually are resisting.

Imagine a twelve-year-old boy walking out the door on a cold day wearing only a T-shirt. His mother says, "Aaron, please put on a sweater. It is cold." She's just trying to stop him from freezing and maybe even getting sick, but he glares at her and slouches off, with the sweater she has given him shoved under his arm.

What do you think Aaron is thinking? *Mom is thoughtful and caring?* Or, could it be:

> *"Mom is being bossy and controlling."*
> *"Mom thinks I'm stupid – that I can't figure out for myself if I'm cold or not. (She has no faith in my judgment.)"*
> *"Why can't she just mind her own business?"*

WHEN THE CHILD DOMINATES: TWO TYPES OF PUSHOVER PARENTS

Say you've just had dinner, and your child hasn't taken the dishes to the kitchen as she promised she would. You ask, and ask again. Nothing happens. So you do it yourself, even though you resent doing your child's job – it's just faster and easier that way. Here's another situation. You're in a restaurant with your seven-year-old son and he's asking, repeatedly, for a second scoop of ice cream. You don't want him to have it on top of the chocolate delight he's already inhaled, but you eventually give in. Better that than endure another embarrassing outburst and showdown in public.

Who has the power in this scenario? The child. Parents hand power over to their children in two major ways: as Permissive Pushovers or Pampering Pushovers.

The Permissive Pushover

It's not difficult to adopt this style, even for those of us who play the superior in other situations. When we do, we end up letting our children rule the roost, not because we want to, but because we feel we don't have a choice. We give in; it's easier than having another argument. The parents in the restaurant are walking on eggshells because they want to avoid a screaming fit. The parent who cleans up the dishes is doing her child's job because she thinks it's easier than badgering the child to take a few dishes off the table, which the parent has already done innumerable times in the past. Either way, the child has the power, and he or she knows it. And we, as parents, are most likely simmering with resentment.

In other words, we've fallen into a very common trap. We've adopted a pushover style, the opposite of the controlling style. We're abdicating our role as the teachers and guides of our children. Many of us end up with this style of parenting at some point. Sometimes it's because we're afraid our child will love us a little less if we say no. We can't stand that possibility, so we say yes every time. If this sounds like you, ask yourself this question: How is that working? If you're seeking love from your child this way, are you getting it?

Some parents say they swing like a pendulum between the controlling style and the pushover style, depending on their mood and the situation. For example, one moment they lay down the law, and the next, when the child resists their efforts, they cave in with exasperation. It's not a comfortable position. It can make us feel bankrupt and powerless. Like failures. As we are the ones who give in most of the time, we start to feel like resentful and unwilling servants. Here's what this sounds like:

> *"Do what you want. I'm tired of fighting with you!"*
> *"You forgot your backpack again? Great, now we have to go back, and I'm going to be late for work again. I hope you're happy."*
> *"Okay, okay, one more TV show. Just stop the whining! And don't think this means you can watch this much tomorrow."*
> *"Okay, just one more scoop of ice cream – but that's it!"*
> *"I did your dishes for you tonight, but this is the last time! I'm not doing them anymore."*

The Pampering Pushover

Let's look at the other common way we give power to our child. Some of us aren't permissive pushovers; we're *pampering* pushovers. We are happy and eager to do things for our child; we even see it as our job. We overserve, overprotect, overdo – from tying a son's shoes at age eight to making his breakfast and packing a lunch for him before he goes to high school. We're even happy to admit that we're pampering our little prince or princess. Doesn't he deserve the best? Perhaps we're at work ten hours a day and feel it's the least we can do when we get home.

"I thought you were putting away your toys, honey. There's no time now; up you go and get ready for bed. I'll do this."
"No, I don't want you pouring the juice; you might make a spill. I'll pour it for you."
"It's already twenty minutes past your bedtime. So I'll read one more story, but you have to promise to go to sleep right after."
"No, I don't want you to climb the monkey bars. You might fall."
"Oh, you don't want the French toast I made this morning? Okay, how about scrambled eggs? No? How about baked Alaska?"
"Here, let me pack your backpack – I can do it for you so your project doesn't get squished – be careful!"

The pampering parent feels happy as she does too much for her child, while the permissive parent resents it. Either way, the child is the boss. The child holds all the cards, and has too much power over both the parent and the situation.

Let's look at the impact of a pampering pushover on a child. In our workshops, we ask parents to play the role of the domineering child. Some feel good to have all the power: *I got my way. I'm in control.* But others feel inadequate or inferior, sometimes suffocated, when the parent does everything for them. And when we talk to people who have grown up under this style of parenting, they wish it had been different: *If my parents had really loved me, they would have set some boundaries and wouldn't have been so concerned about pleasing me. They would have said no sometimes.*

Parents who adopt the pushover style, whether they are permissive or pampering, are not parenting for the long term. How will rescuing children over and over again help them to develop responsibility and resilience? How will saying yes to their every whim help them to be resourceful and respectful? If you choose to pamper your children, you might be able to buy short-term peace, but it will affect the attitudes and skills that they develop over the long term. Children raised this way can end up being irresponsible, disrespectful of others, and insensitive to the needs of the situation. Having learned to manipulate parents, they go on to manipulate friends and other people. It's all about them. It's always been that way at home. Now they feel entitled to get whatever they want.

If we give our children all the power when they're young, we probably won't establish or follow through on limits – especially once they're teenagers and they're pressing us to let them stay out until the early hours of the morning. This ends up slipping into a "do what you want" approach.

We can be sure that children will interpret our words in their own way. Which interpretation would you be pleased with?

"Look what I can get away with!"
"I can get Mom to do anything I want."
"My parents don't care about me or have any interest in what I do."
"My parents believe I can handle my own situation."

Whether their interpretation is accurate or completely unjustified, what children believe will impact their self-esteem – the story they tell themselves about themselves. Unless the parenting they receive consistently prompts that fourth interpretation, they may come to the erroneous conclusion that they're not valued by their parents.

WHEN PARENTS AND CHILDREN ESTABLISH A PARTNERSHIP

THE GUIDING PARENT

Guiding parents do not set rules in stone or play the controller who lords it over their children and tell them what to do. Neither do they cave in to their every whim. Instead, they cooperate and collaborate with their children to solve problems and create solutions. They work in partnership with their kids, on the basis of their long-term parenting goals.

This partnership is based on an approach to everyday living that embraces and incorporates the LRB principles described in chapter 2:

- Unconditional **love**, no matter how children behave
- **Respect** for children's ability to make choices and do things
- **Belief** that children can manage and handle the outcome of their decisions

What does this mean for us, as parents?

The guiding parent is a coach, a teacher, a consultant, and a partner. We do not tell our child what to do or enforce strict rules, partly because we know that in practice we can't force a child, or anyone, to do what we say. Children learn this very quickly and use it to their full advantage. We couldn't force our toddlers to eat certain foods, use the potty, or go to sleep. We also can't force a twelve-year-old to do his homework or make an eight-year-old feel sorry when we make her apologize.

WHAT RESPECT LOOKS LIKE

Respect means that we offer choices within limits. Our child has a say in what goes on within limits appropriate for his or her age or stage of development. We respect our child's ability to explore and decide on many things for himself, and we also let him experience the various outcomes of his choices, knowing he will learn. When guiding our young children, we say, "This is what I think and feel, but I don't want to decide for you. Decide what you think is best." Then we step back, and, unless the situation has a serious risk, we resist the impulse to rush in for the save. We show confidence in our child's ability to handle the results of his choice, even if it means he'll have a struggle.

A guiding parent is a leader, not a dictator. As leaders, we create a family atmosphere that's loving and respectful. We express confidence and faith in our children. We support and encourage them to do their best and to use their innate creativity. It's the process of learning, not just the result, that counts.

What does this guiding parent sound like?

"We have Cheerios and raisin bran for breakfast. Which would you prefer?"

"Looks like you're having trouble putting your toys away. Would you like a helper? Would you like me to pick up the soldiers or the Lego?"

"I know you'd like to eat now, but there's no time left for breakfast. You're welcome to get a piece of fruit or a granola bar for the car if that would help."

"I'm taking my coffee to the car – see you there."

When we ask parents in our workshops to play the children of guiding parents, they get it right away: "My parents believe I can handle things. I feel capable and independent. I know I can do it on my own. I feel respected and good about myself."

This style of parenting encourages very different characteristics in our children. It invites children to use their judgment on how to handle a situation. It encourages them to make decisions for themselves, to learn, and to contribute to the family. It encourages them to be creative and think for themselves and not rely on external motivators – such as the fear of disapproval, punishment, and the guilt trip – to do things. Children raised this way will be motivated from the inside by the joy of learning and discovery.

THE PARENTING STYLES IN ACTION

Think about the first hour of your day, as you're getting your children out the door to school. How does it go? Is it a sunny morning, with the children happily sitting down at the kitchen table for breakfast, getting dressed on time, and walking out the door with everything they need in their backpacks? Or does it go like this:

> *"Get up, get dressed, hurry up, it's breakfast time. Leave your sister alone, the brown pants are in the laundry. No, there's no TV right now. Have you walked the dog? We're going to be late. Turn off the TV. I said LEAVE YOUR SISTER ALONE. Eat your breakfast. No, you can't have chocolate-sprinkled sugar explosions. Don't forget your project. I thought you said you were packed for soccer practice already. I'm not washing the brown pants now. You have to ask me before now if you need change for pizza lunch. Let's go, goodbye, have a good day. Leave your sister alone!"*

We've all been there, and it's not fun. It doesn't set our children up for a productive morning at school, and it certainly doesn't put us, the adults, in a good frame of mind as we head to work. Parents tell us they feel exhausted, lousy about their parenting, and stressed out, all before they get to work. There are plenty of hot spots in a parent's day – homework, dinner, and bedtime, for example – but getting the child out the door in the morning is one of the biggest. It's one of the most common everyday issues that parents bring up in our classes.

How do you get your child out the door in the morning? The answer says a lot about the parenting style you use most of the time. Let's compare what each parenting style looks like in the morning.

PARENTING STYLE	SOUNDS LIKE ...	GOAL OF PARENT
Controlling Parent Superior	Demands, orders, blame, rigid rules, coercion: "I am the parent. Do it because I said so!" "It's your own fault you're hungry. If you had just eaten dinner like you were told." "Just let me do it. You're too slow." "If you'd listened the first time I asked, I wouldn't have to yell at you."	Get respect for the parent Order without freedom for child Obedience Perfection Submission of child
Pushover Parent Inferior	A desire to please, lenience, over-involvement, or exasperation: "Off you go, I'll clean up the toys. This is a big job." "Okay, have another cookie, but only this time." "Let me do it. It's my job to look after you." "Do what you want. I'm tired of fighting with you!"	Respect for the child at parent's expense Freedom without order or limits Please the child, avoid tantrums Pamper and serve child, get appreciation Avoid conflict and stress
Guiding Parent Equal	Calmness, flexibility, encouragement: "I respect your right to choose and I believe you can handle the outcome. If it doesn't work out, you can learn from it." "I love you too much to fight. Let's take a break and figure this out when we are both calm." "I want to hear your thoughts. I believe we can come up with a solution we can both live with."	Dual respect – for child and parent Flexibility, freedom within limits, building life skills Model dignity and respect in relationships Cooperation, teamwork

MESSAGE TO CHILD	TOOLS/TACTICS USED	POSSIBLE IMPACT ON CHILD
Love and approval for child are conditional on child's performance Fall in line or get in trouble Your judgment is inferior to mine You are inadequate and incapable I know best You're difficult	Micromanage, impose rules, instill fear, parent tantrums Blame, threats, bribes, ridicule, criticism Punishment for mistakes, rewards for obedience Benevolence but then about-face when no cooperation Teaching child what to think	Causes high stress, anxiety, and depression Stifles innate desire to explore, be creative, take risks Child remains dependent, fearful of mistakes Child may become a pleaser, a perfectionist, or anxious Motivated externally by fear of hurt and a desire to be loved and accepted by others May rebel, seek power, revenge, become angry, bully peers
Love for and approval of parent is conditional on parent's performance You are inadequate and incapable Manipulate others to get your way The world revolves around you Use power over others to get what you want	Coaxing, hovering, smothering, guilt Walk on eggshells, give in Over-indulge, over-serve, over-protect Teaching child to think about self	Child uses innate creativity to manage others Becomes manipulative, tyrannical, irresponsible, and socially incompetent Becomes spoiled, entitled, dependent Becomes self-centered, has an exaggerated sense of importance
Love and approval are unconditional Your voice is valued and you can figure things out We treat each other respectfully in this family You are capable and your contributions are valuable	Attitude of LRB. Closeness is never in question Give child responsibility, use mistakes as an opportunity to learn Let child experience consequences of actions, demonstrate self-respect, address conflict Collaboration, agreements, and rules based on the needs of the situation, family meetings Teaching child how to think	Self-esteem is never in question Invites child to use innate creativity to explore, take risks, develop life skills Child feels unconditionally loved, develops respect, cooperative social skills, becomes responsible for actions Greater independence, feeling of self-worth, better problem-solving skills

THE CONTROLLING PARENT

To kick this off, we'll dip into the controller's tool kit. Listen for the blame, threats, and commands:

> *"How many times have I told you there's no TV in the morning. Turn it off now! And I don't want to hear any more arguments."*
>
> *"You still haven't got your backpack ready. What is the matter with you?"*
>
> *"Put your mitts on, or your hands will get cold today. No, it's not a choice."*

If you were the child, would you feel like cooperating? Probably not. When we behave like the boss, we create big problems for ourselves. We're giving our children two choices – submit to our demands or take us on. If our relationship with our child is driven by who has the power, getting out the door will be a prime battleground. Why? We're pressed for time. We want to get our children to school on time, and we have a meeting scheduled at work. We desperately need our children to cooperate.

And don't they know it! This is the moment when they choose to fuss over their clothes, or look for the hockey stick they somehow lost, or stay in their pajamas until three minutes before leaving time, or just dawdle as only a child knows how.

THE PUSHOVER PARENT

When a parent is permissive or pampers the child, the child is clearly the boss:

"Okay, okay. Watch some TV. Just stop the whining. And don't think that means you can watch any tomorrow."
"You're so slow. Here, let me handle your pack – just get your coat on. We're going to be late again!"
"Don't worry, Daddy will carry your mitts for you. I'll have them here if your hands get cold."

So what is this child likely thinking and feeling? Probably *I can get my way if I hold out long enough.* A parent who is a permissive pushover reinforces in the child the idea that power is where it's at and feeds their feelings of joy when they win. A child who becomes accustomed to using power and control over others can easily start to bully their peers. If we're pampering, the child may feel entitled and become spoiled.

In both cases children can become manipulative, selfish, and self-centered. They aren't learning how to respect and consider others.

THE GUIDING PARENT

On a good day, when we're rested and in a better frame of mind, we can sound more like this:

"When is it that we watch TV in our house?"
"You know, I could use some help in here. Do you want to be in charge of pouring the juice for breakfast or flipping the pancakes?"
"It's five minutes to leaving time. Is there anything you need to do before we go?"

"Would you prefer to wear your mitts today or put them in your pack for later?"

This is how a guiding parent starts the day. Let's take a closer look at what's going on here. First, we get our child to focus on the needs of the situation – what needs to be done now. "It's five minutes to leaving time." This just states the fact, gives information. "Is there anything you need to do?" We are not telling our child what to do, as in: "Hurry up and get your books from upstairs." Instead, we leave it to the child to tell himself what to do. *Oh yeah, I need to get my backpack ready. I'd better go and do that now.*

You're probably thinking, *Yeah, right! My child wouldn't make that leap.* And you may be correct – it may not happen right away. Children need training to learn a new way. It can take time for them to make the shift. But it's important to get started.

It's not just what we say, either. It's how we say it. Our tone of voice and even our posture will send out a clear message about what we really think and how we really feel. This is why it's so important to believe in, and absorb, the LRB principles of love, respect, and belief and embed them into our daily operating system. So when we say, in an even voice, "Do you have anything left to do?" what we're really saying is:

"My love for you is not in question, even if this morning we end up having a struggle."
"I respect your right to make decisions and act for yourself, even if I don't necessarily agree with your choice."

"I believe that you can figure this out. And, even if you don't manage it very well this time, you'll be able to handle the outcome and learn from it."

And, at the end of the day, which household would you rather grow up in?

MAKING RESPECT A REFLEX ACTION

Most parents would be thrilled to have a pleasant morning with their children before they go out the door. But how do we get there? To start with, we need to override that natural reflex to manage and control the child, to get the child to do what we want. We need to make a conscious decision to do that. For many parents, this is the hardest part. They get stalled, and it's tempting to revert to the default position of protect, manage, and control. But once parents are convinced this is a better way of parenting, it's just a question of learning some skills and filling up their parental tool kit with new techniques that are more respectful.

A word of warning: Kids may take some time to get used to your new approach. Initially, they will be surprised and puzzled by this new behavior, this seemingly new and improved parent. *Is my parent using reverse psychology on me?* Their behavior might even get worse for a while, if only to test how sincere you are. This is actually a good sign. It means they have noticed your valiant effort to change. So don't get discouraged. Persevere, for this, too, will pass.

Planning ahead and creating routines with children is crucial. Being proactive feels so much better than being reactive all the time. You can discuss the situation in advance with your child. Sit down at a quiet and peaceful time and say:

> *"Our mornings haven't been going very well, lately. I've been raising my voice a lot, and today you even left in tears. How are you feeling about our mornings?"*
> Then listen.
> Then say: *"Well, I care too much about our relationship to start our day this way. What do you think would make mornings better?"*

Listen again. Now is the time to get out a pen and paper and together map out a new routine. Let the needs of the situation be the boss and plan around that. "We need to leave for school at 8:15, so what time do you need to get up in the morning to have enough time to have breakfast and get ready? How would you like to wake up? Shall I wake you up, or would you like an alarm clock? Shall we go and buy one for you?"

If breakfast is an issue, the process is the same. If, for example, you don't want your child eating sugary cereal before school, you can give her a couple of options. Perhaps you can agree on one day a week when your child can treat herself to frosted flakes, or the whole family could have it for dessert after dinner.

You're far more likely to win cooperation this way because your child has made a choice about what time she's getting up and how she's going to approach her morning. She might agree to set an alarm clock to get herself up. Now it's up to her to get ready; you're not going to badger her every morning. You might say, "It's ten minutes to leaving time. Is there anything you need to do?"

WHO MANAGES AND HANDLES OUTCOMES?

Here's the tricky part: We respect our child's ability to make decisions and get ready on his own, but, if he doesn't, he will have to manage the outcome. If he doesn't get ready on time, he'll go to school without a warm breakfast and potentially without the proper clothes. Maybe he goes to school with messy hair or unbrushed teeth. This might be uncomfortable for him, but it won't harm him. It might also be uncomfortable for us! It's hard to watch our child go to school this way, but what is the goal? Perfection or improvement? Dependence or independence? It's a learning curve for both of us. He's learning how to manage and handle himself, and we're learning to have faith and confidence in his ability to do so.

Let's see how the guiding parent handles some typical morning situations. Here is respect in action:

1. Your child asks for bacon and eggs on a rushed school morning.
   You can say, *"Wouldn't that be nice, but there's no time today. So what would you prefer, a toasted bagel or a bowl of cereal? You choose."*
   (Respect = giving the child a choice.)

2. Your child fools around and doesn't eat breakfast and now it's time to go.
   You can say, *"Unfortunately, there's no time left for breakfast. Would you like to help yourself to an apple or a granola bar for the car?"*
   (Respect = letting the needs of the situation be the boss and giving the child a choice.)
3. Your child can't find his skates/running shoes/ballet slippers for school.
   You can say, *"They might be in the front hall closet or the mud room, if you want to take a look there."*
   (Respect = giving information, not doing for a child what he can do for herself.)
4. It's time to go and your child isn't ready.
   You can say, *"I'm getting my coat on. I'll meet you at the door."*
   (Respect = telling the child what you will do, not what they will do.)

A guiding parent does not say to a six-year-old, "If you don't hurry up, I'm leaving without you."

A threat can inject a shot of anxiety or fear into a young child. It also sends the message that the parent is not confident that the child can be cooperative without some external motivation or pressure. Even if it might make her hurry up in the short term, it can cause long-term ripples by making her feel insecure and unsure of her parents' love for her.

5. Your child refuses to wear mitts on a cold day.
   You might say, *"It's cold outside today. If you don't feel like wearing your mitts, would you like to tuck them in your pack for later?"*
6. Your child still isn't dressed and now it's time to go.
   You can say, *"It's leaving time. We'll need to take your clothes with us, and you can get dressed in the car or when we get there."*

This last option is effective. It won't be very comfortable, but it won't hurt, and, in most cases, it won't happen again. We know this isn't easy for parents. Understandably you want your child to be ready for school, with pencils sharpened and clothes clean. But we urge you to follow through. He won't suffer any lasting harm if he arrives at school a day or two with messy clothes and hair, or no breakfast in his tummy. But he is totally capable of learning from it and seeing that he can handle the outcome of his choices. He'll also learn that you have confidence that he can manage it, too.

CHANGING PATTERNS

Changing old patterns takes time and practice, especially since we probably developed these patterns during our formative years, at a time when parents just told children what to do and expected them to obey. Our human instinct is to protect by controlling and managing. So we are breaking new ground, and it's like learning any new skill, be it a new golf swing or a new piece

MAGIC BULLET
Belief in Action

True stories from our parenting classes:

One dad took his daughter to school in her pajamas. After that morning, he says, he never had trouble getting her, or any of her siblings (who were not even born at that time!) out the door.

Another parent says his four-year-old daughter refused to put on clothes, any clothes, one morning. "I don't need clothes," she said. The parent decided to go with it. He put on his coat and opened the door. The little girl ventured to the door, and to his relief, quickly turned back and put on her clothes. Now, obviously the parent wouldn't have let his daughter go to school naked, but the point is that when given some space, the little girl quickly came to her own conclusion.

A mom did not believe her three-year-old daughter when she said it was pajama day at nursery school the next day. Surely the teacher would have sent a note home! The mom's first instinct was to insist that her daughter get dressed as usual, as she did not want her to be embarrassed. Resisting her desire to protect her child, the mom let her daughter get in her spouse's car in her pajamas, carrying a bag of clothes. When she got to work, her spouse called her and said, "Guess what? It's pajama day." The mom had tears in her eyes as she told this story to the class.

on the piano. It will take some time and lots of practice. We're bound to struggle, so we need to cut ourselves some slack and be patient.

OUR OWN PARENTING JOURNEY

We both started the traditional way, as controlling parents. We wanted to show our children the best way forward and help them avoid some of the pitfalls that we experienced in our youth. Then we found ourselves issuing orders because we thought that was the only way we could make them safe and successful in the future. It wasn't working very well. We did our share of controlling, managing, and directing, and neither of us felt very good about it.

Instead of handing out unsolicited advice, we focused on what we could do and say that would build on our children's core strengths so they could live safe and fulfilling lives. Our aim was to make them feel confident enough to make choices for themselves and be responsible for the outcome, whatever it was. We wanted to make sure they knew we loved them, no matter how they performed. This, we hoped, would give them a solid foundation for the future.

BEVERLEY

When my daughter, Kate, was two, we locked horns all day long. It was a miserable life for both of us. I'd say, "Come on, honey, let's get ready for nursery school." She'd say, "I'm not going." I couldn't get her into the bathtub. I couldn't get her out. When I'd make spaghetti, her favorite dinner, she'd say, "You make yucky dinners." It was really sad for both of us.

It started the day her brother, Andrew, was born. Kate felt dethroned and forgotten. On the second day he was home, she wanted him to go back to wherever he came from. Then she started to retaliate. She'd knock things off his change table and shake his crib. It wasn't safe to leave them alone together.

The most important thing I had to do for Kate was to show her that she was loved, no matter what. She had come to the mistaken conclusion that she was not loved, and it made her terribly hurt and unhappy. Everyone could see it. She wore a scowl on her face every day. I realized that I had also labeled her in my mind – every morning I was on guard for the next disruption. I thought of her as difficult and miserable to be with.

That's when I registered for a parenting course with Dr. Martin Nash and his wonderful wife, Georgine. With their caring guidance, I learned how to reach my daughter and provide her with a new snapshot of herself. Each day I told her that I loved her, no matter what, and that we were so lucky she was born in our family. Then I treated her as if she were already where I wanted her to be – cooperative and happy. At night I started to massage her back and sing her a new lullaby, "Where are you going, my happy one, little one?" When she first heard the word *happy*, she stiffened, and on the third night she said in a wee voice, "Mummy, do you really think I'm your happy one?" I knew then I was breaking through.

Kate had been hanging on to the idea that she was difficult

and rejected. Once she believed that she was accepted and loved, people couldn't believe the change in her. When she knew she was loved, the need to fight went out of her. We became a team instead of adversaries.

DOONE

My kids were sixteen, thirteen, eleven, and eight when I changed my ways. I used to rattle off a string of directives: "Where's your backpack? Where's your lunch? Please do your hair and brush your teeth. Leave your brother alone. There's no TV at breakfast. Come on, let's go, it's late!"

Then I decided to change tactics. Instead, I made a concerted effort to say to each child, "Good morning, sweetie, how are you?" Instead of issuing constant reminders, I poured myself a coffee and said, "It's such a nice day. Does everybody have everything they need? See you in the car in ten minutes."

It was a real challenge for me to hold my tongue, but pretty soon, the kids stopped resisting and talking back. It was actually funny to see the four of them running around the house so they wouldn't be the last one to leave. Even the dawdler would get in the car without nagging – as we were pulling out the driveway.

I used to run around trying to monitor the screens in the house – TV screens, computers, games, cell phones. I would go from one child to the next saying, "Turn off the show. It's homework time." They'd say, "It's not a show, it's a game. I just have to get to the next level." Or, "I just have to finish this Facebook post." Then I'd go back to the first one, and, sure enough, another screen was on.

Then I stopped trying to turn off the screens. Instead, I'd say, "What's your plan for the evening? What's your homework and screen strategy tonight? How are you going to fit all of this around your sports practice schedule?" We stopped arguing about the screens, and they became more responsible. They were more in control of the process and responded accordingly.

CHANGING OUR BEHAVIOR

Something funny happened when we changed our behavior in this way. Our children's reactions and their behavior also changed. We argued less, and we felt less need to manage or scold our kids. The more respectfully we treated our children, the more respectfully they responded. We created an upward spiral. Perhaps it's not that surprising. Kids who feel worthy and loved and confident don't tend to lash out at their parents. Kids who have the freedom to choose (within limits appropriate for their age) don't have to rebel to carve out some freedom for themselves.

But for parents to change their behavior, they need to understand it first, a subject we turn to in the next chapter.

EXERCISE: PARENTING STYLE SELF-TEST

Take this test to understand the difference between controlling, pushover (permissive/pampering), and guiding leadership.

1. You are talking to a friend. Your child enters the room to play. His play becomes noisy. You can:

   a) Yell at him to keep quiet.

   b) Tell him he is disturbing you, then ignore him and talk louder.

   c) Tell him he is disturbing you and giving him a choice of playing quietly or going to another room to play.

2. On wash day you find eight-year-old Kim's dirty clothes on the floor in her room instead of in the hamper where she had agreed to put them. You can:

   a) Pick up the clothes and wash them anyway because you know she was in a hurry to get to the Wii.

   b) Storm into the family room, switch off the Wii, and demand that Kim pick up her clothes immediately.

   c) Leave the clothes and wash only what is in the hamper.

3. Mom and six-year-old Ahmed are at the store. He wants a chocolate bar, but his allowance is all used up. Mom can:

   a) Buy him a chocolate bar to avoid a fuss.

b) Tell him she understands how nice it would be to have a chocolate bar right now, but that he has already chosen how to spend his allowance.

c) Give him a lecture on the value of his money and tell him he should know better than to ask for more.

Scoring Key
1a, 2b, 3c are controlling parenting tools
1b, 2a, 3a are pushover tactics
1c, 2c, 3b are guiding approaches

Action Planning: Answer the following questions. Reflections like these contribute to deeper learning.

What is your dominant parenting style?

How did you come to adopt this style? (e.g., childhood experience, personal approach to relationships, or beliefs about yourself, others, and the role of a parent)

What changes would you like to make?

What do you require to help you make these changes? (e.g., information, support, skills, shift in beliefs)

What are some of the roadblocks to being the parent that you want to be?

It's Your Default: Why Parents Act the Way They Do

Cave Parent: *"If you don't hurry up, the saber-toothed tiger is going to get you and eat you for dinner! I mean it. Do you see it coming down the hill? Get inside the cave NOW. I can't believe I have to tell you this every day. I'm going to go gray over you!"*

Today's Parent: *"If you don't hurry up, you are going to miss the bus and be late for school! I mean it. Do you see it coming down the hill? Get outside NOW. I can't believe I have to tell you this every day. I'm going to go gray over you!"*

Cave Parent: *"Why are you in here playing your pebbles game? You're supposed to be outside doing your homework and learning how to set this tiger trap. Get going right now or you're not going to have supper, you're going to* ***be*** *supper!"*

Today's Parent: *"Why are you in here playing your computer games? You have to do your homework and learn the times tables for your test. Get going right now or you're never going to be able to get a job and put supper on the table!"*

It is ironic that we parents often act as though we were still in prehistoric times, reacting protectively to our children's behavior as if they are in a life or death situation. To understand how to overcome this, we need to delve a little deeper into the origins and fundamental drivers of our behavior. Psychologists call these deep emotional impulses *systems of motivation*. They affect the way we relate to our kids, our friends, our colleagues, and our spouse, yet they're so deeply embedded in us that we might not even notice them.

OUR FIRST NATURE: PROTECTING BY MANAGING AND CONTROLLING

This is our primal nature, more than two billion years old; to be successful, to be a winner, to be superior. Success was getting supper; failure was being supper. When we become parents, our instinct tells us to protect our young ones by managing and controlling them. In ancient times, the survival of children depended on their obedience and submissiveness to their parents and elders.

We are all born with this drive to avoid all hurts, both physical and emotional. The most obvious solution is to be superior in all situations: Never be a failure or a loser. It comes with the package of being human! We can see it operating today in all aspects of life:

- Success vs. failure
- Win vs. lose

- Superior vs. inferior
- Dominant vs. submissive
- Master vs. servant

This instinct is driven by powerful emotions. When we win, when we're superior, we feel thrilled and joyful. When we lose, when we're inferior, we feel hurt and humiliated. The primal nature's main function is to help us avoid being physically hurt. It is our default position. When we touch a hot stove, for instance, we recoil without thinking about it. So it's not surprising that this automatic, involuntary reflex to avoid hurt for ourselves and our loved ones is central to our parenting.

This reflex drives us to tell our kids what to do. "I'm the parent. I know better, so do what you're told. If you follow my advice, you'll avoid being hurt." This is the controlling style of parenting that so many of us knew when we were children.

Why do parents slip into it so easily, even now? It gives us, as parents, pleasure to see our child do well. We want to show our kids the tried and true way to happiness and success. We don't want them to struggle.

But this approach is also rooted in fear – the fear, by definition, of getting hurt in the future. We think controlling our child and telling him what to do will keep him safe and ensure him a healthy and happy future. In our brain it's all about the future. So when we see our son watching TV on Saturday afternoon, we think, *If I don't step in, he'll watch TV all day, all weekend, all summer, and he'll never stop watching! What will happen to him in the future?*

Or if our twelve-year-old daughter steals twenty dollars from our purse to spend at the mall, we think, *If she's doing this now, at age twelve, what will she be doing at eighteen? Will she end up in jail? Where is this leading?*

Parents have a vivid imagination when it comes to their children. They can easily predict that the very worst outcome will occur, so they act accordingly in the present moment by managing and controlling their child. Yet most parents are only dimly aware, when they issue orders and warnings, that they are reacting in the present to a future that most likely will never occur.

MAGIC BULLET
Fear

Fear is rampant in today's parenting.

We help parents recognize that the majority of the interactions they have with their children are over issues that are not life-threatening. We help them determine which situations are actually dangerous. For example, many parents struggle with children over whether they will wear mitts on a cold winter's day. We suggest letting nature teach the child that he will feel cold when he doesn't cover his hands.

Focus on the big picture, the long term, and remind yourself that parenting out of fear stunts growth. Remember that making changes takes time and you will probably slip back to your familiar parenting style when you're scared.

For children to learn resilience and responsibility, they need to be exposed to opportunities and challenges. If parents remove all obstacles for their children, they won't learn how to handle things on their own. We do a disservice to our children when we do too much for them.

What's the Other Option?

One of our jobs as parents is to protect our children. Sometimes, however, helping them build immunity by exposing them to certain risks is the best protection.

Letting them take their first step, whether as toddlers in the living room, as kindergarteners into the classroom, as tweens onto the subway, or teenagers going off to university, is a risk all parents face.

Here are some ways to ease the transition:

1. Do not do for your child what she is capable of doing. If we do too much for our children, we risk robbing them of the sense of accomplishment they get when they do it themselves.

2. Let your children handle as many challenges as possible in their daily lives. They will become more confident, resilient, and independent as a result. Often we parent for the short term, stickhandling for our children now and hoping they learn later. Our job is to teach them coping skills, and the sooner they learn, the better off they will be.

3. Take comfort in knowing that even if your child is unhappy sometimes, he is learning that uncomfortable feelings can be sustained, dealt with, and

eventually overcome. This holds true for many feelings, such as loneliness, embarrassment, frustration, and anger. A parent's role in many of these situations is to be empathetic and supportive, not to "fix it."

4. Help your child problem solve without giving your preferred solution too soon. Explore various options and the consequences of each. Be supportive when their choices do not work out. This is not the time to say "I told you so." Your child will have learned a valuable lesson and gained a tool to use in future similar situations.
5. Make sure you look after yourself. A happy, confident parent is one of the best indicators of a successful child! After all, it's great modeling.

OUR SECOND NATURE: NURTURING BY EXPLORING, CREATING, AND SHARING

Our second nature, which is more recently evolved and therefore inherently less strong, focuses not only on the end product of success and survival but also on the process: learning, exploring, and being creative. We seek to satisfy our curiosity and to understand and predict the future. We do our best, but we are also aware that mistakes are not only inevitable but sometimes very useful. They're an opportunity to learn more. We all get a kick out of our successes, but in this second nature, we don't stay disappointed or hurt when we're not successful. We also strive to share with and help our loved ones and society.

We don't want to eliminate or diminish the joy of winning, of course. But, as many athletes know, you are more likely to be successful if you focus on the process of doing your best, meeting the needs of a given moment, and letting go of the fear of losing. You're more likely to succeed at work if you get into a relaxed but alert headspace when you need to create something new, instead of starting off by thinking, "Oh boy, I better come up with something brilliant by ten o'clock this morning!" It's the excitement of this process, not just the winning, that counts.

The two motivational systems that propel our behavior are:

- Protecting from potential hurts by managing and controlling
- Nurturing the process of exploring, learning, creating, and sharing

These deep impulses drive the way we relate to our children. And they drive the way our children relate to us. It's interesting that we need both to survive. Life is a constant choice of which nature we will draw from. When the situation is potentially threatening to life or limb, our reflex of stress and fear will kick in, leading to a need to protect by taking control. When the situation is not life-threatening, we have the choice to explore and share. This is where things get murky, though. We live in different times. Research has shown children in the developed world have never been safer. Yet when they make a mistake, we still have that ancient reflex to disapprove and punish, to warn against mistakes – even in those moments that aren't life-threatening. Next time you go there, you can blame it on Mother Nature.

To determine which nature we are operating in, we might ask ourselves, *Is it possible that I told or even ordered my child to do something in a way that didn't respect his judgment? Even if I thought it was for his own good? Am I possibly stifling his creativity?* If the answer is yes, we may have inadvertently hurt our child, sometimes very deeply.

This may be surprising. After all, when we offered that advice or made that order, weren't we just trying to be a good parent? Yet if we tell a child what to do, what we're really saying is, "You don't have the judgment to deal with this issue. Therefore, you can't have a voice or a say in your life right now – even if the question is just whether you should wear a sweater on a cool October morning." Kids have a deep desire and need to grow and explore and learn from their own experiences, whether successful or not. If we continue to tell them what to do, even if we feel it's for their own good, we may be sending the message that we think they're not capable or competent.

Let's hear what this sounds like. An eight-year-old is getting ready to go to school on a wet day.

Parent: "It's raining today, so you better wear your raincoat."
Child thinks: "It's not raining that hard, and I don't want to wear my raincoat."

Moments later, Dad repeats the message. "Don't forget, it's raining. You're going to need your raincoat."

Child thinks: "Okay already. I heard you the first time, and I still don't want to wear it."

As the child is getting ready to go out the door, Dad says, "I said, get your raincoat!"

The child now thinks, "Stop ordering me around. I don't want to wear it, and you can't make me! And I am going to show you by kicking the cat!"

When children feel disrespected, they'll resist us or even lash out in one way or another. Some children may even refuse to take their raincoats, knowing they'll get soaking wet, just to show you that you're not the boss of them.

What can we do? Change not only takes time, but requires repetition, practice, and reinforcement. As we have emphasized, the challenge is to harness each of these opposing natures effectively. It's a unique focus and one that truly helps parents make the change they need to reach their goals. When we adopt this approach, we usually find that our child's behavior improves dramatically. Why? He has nothing to defy or rebel against.

EXERCISE: CONSIDER BEFORE YOU REACT

Parenting experts Jane Nelson and Lynn Lott have developed a series of questions for parents who want to slow down and think before they react to their children's behavior. These questions move a parent from fear-based thinking to reflecting on their long-term goals, the motivation behind their child's behavior, and the ways to approach situations cooperatively with the child. The following exercise is modeled on their approach.
Ask yourself:

1. Are we in saber-toothed tiger territory here or not?

2. What lessons are most important for my child to learn in this situation?

3. Am I parenting to get through the day or for the long term?

4. Am I expecting too much from my child, given his age and experience? Is it my patience that is wearing thin?

5. If I approach this situation as a puzzle, what can I figure out about my child's current emotional situation? Is he tired, frustrated or hurting?

6. Has my approach contributed a piece to this puzzle? Are my tone and facial expressions getting the better of me?

7. If I change my perception to see this situation as a problem-solving opportunity, how can I involve my child in finding a solution?

Cooperation Basics:

- Know that another "child behavior puzzle" will present itself sooner or later.
- Be ready with your tools.
- Prioritize Tiger Territory - don't sweat the small stuff.

Ain't Misbehavin': Why Kids Act the Way They Do

We've looked at why parents act the way they do. What about kids? What's behind their actions?

There is a reason for every behavior and misbehavior. Each one has a purpose. When children dawdle, when they refuse to pick up their clothes covering the floor, or when they punch their little brother, they do it for a reason. They may not be aware of the reason, but it's there under the surface, and it is our job, as parents, to figure it out. If we ask a young child why they did something, they will honestly say they don't know. Once we determine what's driving our children's behavior, we'll know what to do in the moment.

Why do children behave the way they do?

Our inspiration comes from Rudolf Dreikurs, one of America's foremost psychiatrists and educators. Born in

Vienna in 1897, Dreikurs studied psychiatrist Alfred Adler's system of Individual Psychology and turned it into a practical method of understanding why children misbehave. His book *Children: The Challenge* shows parents like us how to encourage cooperative behavior without punishment or reward.

From day one, our children's brains and thought processes are developing. Their brains, made up of a hundred billion cells, are super computers helping them to make heads or tails out of all the stimuli and situations that they're experiencing. Unlike computers, however, children's brains have a very powerful emotional component. They feel joy and hurt, and they come up with their own interpretation of what is happening. This is where it can get tricky for us as parents. We cannot control the way our children interpret the world. We can only correct them after the fact, and only if we have taken the time and effort to understand their point of view.

It's easy to understand how children can feel hurt when they fall off their bikes or the monkey bars at the park. What's harder for us to understand are the psychological hurts – mainly those that come from a sense of failure or from a diminishment of love and approval within their family and other social groups.

When children feel joy and love, their behavior will be cooperative and useful. When they feel hurt, possibly as a result of their own interpretations and conclusions, they tend to be uncooperative and rebellious. When children feel hurt inside, they feel justified in hurting others, or "hurting out."

THE HURTS BEHIND MISBEHAVIOR: THE THREE P'S

If our child is acting out, it's our job as parents to figure out why. We know that our child feels hurt, but what can we do? Do we have to be a Sherlock Holmes to figure it out? No. Luckily, the answer is close at hand. Children usually feel hurt for one or more of three reasons: performance, people, and prediction.

PERFORMANCE

Children feel hurt when they conclude that they are failures or not good enough. Children sometimes judge their own performance and give it an F. We know children who will bring home 80 percent on a test and be down on themselves. They don't feel good enough.

We all feel hurt when we're disappointed in our performance; what's damaging is when we attach our worth to our performance. When a child does this, he believes his performance = his worth. How could this be? He may have absorbed the idea that life is about winning or losing, about success or failure, about being on top or being inferior, and he has come out a loser in his mind. It's a bad place to be, because he can lose his confidence and belief in himself. This is what is behind a child's self-esteem going up and down like a yo-yo.

PEOPLE

Children feel hurt when they do not believe they have the love and approval, in a given moment, of their family or important peer groups. They feel rejected. This can easily happen when people in a child's life are focused on performance and success. Many parents naturally prod their children to succeed – at school, on the sports field, in the studio, on stage. We often show our pleasure when they succeed and our disappointment when they don't. The child quickly gets the message: How well I perform = how much I am loved and accepted. This can set children up for a lifetime of insecurity. They will always be on guard and worry, both that they are inadequate and that their social acceptability is at risk.

PREDICTION

The thunderbolt strikes. The child never saw it coming. Out of the blue something happens that she hadn't expected, hadn't predicted. It might seem like something minor to an adult, but to a ten-year-old girl, not being invited to a birthday party is a big deal and very hurtful. What made it a thunderbolt hurt, though, was that she had already made the birthday card for her friend and believed that she was going to be invited. Lots of people can disappoint or betray us, but what really hurts is when our own predictions and judgments betray us.

THE THREE MAIN PURPOSES BEHIND A CHILD'S MISBEHAVIOR

We have discussed the value of detecting which of the three main hurts may be behind a child's misbehavior (problems associated with performance, people, and prediction). Now let's turn, in the

MAGIC BULLET
The Choice Around Hurt

Even though it is our reflex to be hurt when we are rejected, when we feel like failures, or when something unexpected happens to us, we do have a choice. When it comes to these emotional hurts, we determine how long we will stay hurt. We can carry our hurts around with us for the rest of our lives, or we can let them go within moments. The choice is ours. The key is to be aware that we have this choice not to stay hurt.

rest of this chapter, to the three main *purposes* behind their misbehavior: seeking proof of love, respect, and belief.

1. SEEKING PROOF OF LOVE

Children want the same things we all want – safety and security, unconditional love and approval, respect and value. If they have these things, they will have less reason to rebel. When they feel loved and respected, they will have the confidence to handle whatever comes their way.

However, if children feel that their parents' love is conditional, respect is variable, and belief is hedged, they will feel hurt and insecure and may rebel and misbehave.

Every misbehaving child is a hurt and discouraged child, and it is our job, as parents, to understand the source of this discouragement and to treat them with compassion.

It is usually easy to figure out why newborns are upset.

Often it's for physical reasons. They're crying because they're hungry, tired, sick, cold, hot, or wet. When we feed them, change their diaper, and offer kisses, hugs, and a soothing voice, we help them feel happy and comfortable. But, as they get older, the source of their upsets can expand and they can become discouraged. If we look at what our child is doing and tune into our own thoughts and feelings, we have a good shot at knowing the purpose of the behavior and what we should do about it.

When a child thinks that she is loved and approved of by her parents only when certain conditions are met, she'll be hurt. Then she'll seek proof, in different ways, that she is loved. If we're lucky, she'll use her words first to check out her assumptions by asking questions like, "Mommy, don't you love me right now?" or, "Do you love my sister more than me?" This will give us the opportunity to correct her interpretation. If we're unlucky, she'll act out instead. This initially happens in one of two forms: demands for our attention and attempts to keep us in her service.

You've just picked up your four-year-old from school and have had a nice chat with her on the way home. As you walk in the door, the phone rings. It's a friend you haven't talked to in ages. But your four-year-old starts tugging at your sweater: "Mummy, mummy!" You try to ignore her, but it doesn't work.

Now she's screaming, "Mummy, mummy, I need to talk to you!" You apologize to your friend and hang up the phone.

"What is it now?" you ask.

"There's an ant on my pencil."

It's a common scenario; kids interrupt when their parents are conversing with another adult. Then, once they've got your attention, they're temporarily satisfied and will go back to their activities – until the next need for reassurance arises. This behavior is much more common in children under five, and it tends to increase when a new brother or sister arrives on the scene.

In our classes, we help parents understand what's happening by asking them to play out the scene. Some parents are assigned the role of the parent on the phone, while others play the four-year-old who wants attention. After thirty seconds – during which the parents acting as children usually do an outstanding job of whining and pestering – we ask everyone how they feel. The parents on the phone usually say they feel annoyed, frustrated, irritated. They find themselves reminding, coaxing, and finally snapping at the children. The children say they feel left out, ignored, even desperate, but when the parents give in, they feel happy, because they got the attention and proof that they wanted. The children even say they feel like they're playing a game where one person wins and the other loses.

So what's happening?

It makes no logical sense to parents that a child who has enjoyed our undivided attention all morning becomes intensely demanding the moment we're on the phone or we stop to chat for a minute with a neighbor.

But things look different from a child's point of view. Kids want to feel connected, and all of a sudden if we pick up the phone or see a friend in the grocery store, we're not available to them. To them, the connection is broken, and they don't like it. That's why, when you re-establish the connection after putting down the phone, they go back to whatever they were doing.

Something deeper may be going on: they may be questioning whether we love them unconditionally. The answer may seem obvious to us. Of course we love our children. But they want proof.

When they are age two, kids crave their parents' attention, that physical demonstration of their love. They haven't learned yet that their parents can still love them even when they're talking to someone else. They can't appreciate that yet. Life for a preschooler is black and white. Love is either being given, or it's gone. If we're not available, the child can believe that they've lost that love connection with us. He or she may feel left out, ignored, and unloved.

Then the child might think, *I count only when I'm being noticed* or *I'm only important when I'm keeping you busy with me.*

The child, in other words, has come up with the mistaken belief that Time = Love. They are measuring. *The more time you spend with me, the more I feel loved.* Conversely, *The more time you spend with my sibling, the more you love her.* This is a no-win situation for the parent. We won't ever be able to keep things even, and that isn't actually the goal, anyway. A better message for the child is *I love both you and your sister 100 percent. I couldn't love you more. I love you when you're asleep, when you're in my lap reading a book, when I'm at work, and when you've made a mistake. My love for you is not in question.*

If we don't deal with this behavior, it can continue for many years. Even at twelve, kids interrupt when their parents are on the phone, saying things like, "Mom, what shirt do you think I should wear? The pink one or the red one?"

It's an important thing to get right when kids are young. Children need to learn not to interrupt or to say "excuse me" and then wait their turn. They also need to learn how to show regard and respect for others. Therefore, if the parent does not show self-respect and answers the child every time he has a question, children will not learn how to delay gratification or acknowledge the needs of the situation. They may think their own needs are paramount.

If you notice your child is consistently interrupting you, what can you do? Here's what works:

Give information in advance.

You explain to your child, ideally beforehand, that you need to make a call and you don't wish to be interrupted unless it's an emergency. You can say to a young child, "Daddy wants to talk to Grandma this morning, and it's not respectful for me to talk to two people at once. Unless it's an emergency, you need to wait until I'm off the phone to talk to me. I love you, and I'll spend time with you when my call is done." Or, "I'm expecting a call, so I'll be busy for five minutes. What would you like to do while I'm on the phone?" You can also talk about what an emergency is – that the baby has fallen or the sink is overflowing.

Even if you prepare them in advance, children will not always respond cooperatively at first. There can be a testing period, particularly if your child has been successfully interrupting you for a while. Think of this as a training period. If you practice the LRB principles – love, respect and belief – your child will accept the new conditions.

When it has not gone well and your child has tried to interrupt again, you can say,

"I'm off the phone now. What was so important?" or, "I'm all yours now, what did you want?" or, "It can be really hard to be patient and wait your turn. We'll get there. Perhaps it will be easier next time." These words communicate that you still care about your child and you respect her (even when she treats you disrespectfully). You'll also spread the seeds of confidence around her.

Do not stop what you're doing to give your child attention.

This doesn't mean that you brush off your child in a cold way. When the phone rings and your child starts tugging at your sleeve, you might rub her back to let her know you're aware of her presence, without making eye contact. The message is: "I know you're there, but I don't want to be interrupted. I will be all yours shortly."

Redirect your child's attention.

If you have a young child, consider keeping a basket of quiet playthings or some stickers and a little book near the phone. Then you can explain to your child that he is welcome to be near you, but not to interrupt you.

Show respect for your child.

If it's story time and the phone rings, you could say, "It's story time, so I'm not going to take that call." If it's a call you've been waiting for, you could say, "I've been waiting for this call. I'm sorry it's interrupting our story, but I will come back to you as soon as I can."

Separate the deed from the doer.

We make it clear to our children that we love them, no matter what, but that doesn't mean we'll love everything they do. They won't love everything we do, either, but they love us, too.

MAGIC BULLET
Seeking Proof of Love Through Service

Parents in our classes often complain about the child who sucks up all their energy. More often than not, it's their first-born. Very early on, these children master the art of making demands and keeping others in their service, generally at the expense of their siblings. They never get enough attention and service.

Here's how it sounds. "My arms are too tired. Can you do it for me?" or, "But I didn't want my toast cut in squares, I wanted triangles!" or, "But I wanted the blue cup. I don't want the red cup," or, "He got more grapes than I did. That's not fair!"

Do not do for children what they can do for themselves. Acting hopeless or helpless can be their way to manipulate a parent into their service. So surprise them next time and say the unexpected: "I love you too much to do that for you when I know you are capable of doing it for yourself," or, "It would be disrespectful of me to do what you can do for yourself." These responses may elicit a bit of eye rolling from your older child.

There are other ways to seek proof of love. Children show off, behave like a clown at the dinner table or in school, are overly good (and show great pleasure in pointing out that their sibling is not), or have food issues at the table that keep their parent focused on them and not their siblings.

A more covert way of seeking attention can be shyness. This can become a very powerful label for a child. Some parents bend over backwards to get their shy child comfortable in new situations. We promise to stay at birthday parties so that our child will go. We speak for our shy child when he's asked a question. This doesn't help in the long run. It sends the child a strong message: *I don't have confidence in your ability to handle situations.* If you have a budding shy child in these kinds of situations, you can say instead, "When you're ready to join the others, just let me know." Or, "I'm willing to stay at the party for five minutes to help you get settled and then I'll come back when it's over." If this doesn't work for your child, that's all right. You can try again next time. This, too, will pass!

Pass the job on to the child.

The minute a child complains about "the service around here," pass the job to her. Take time for training. "You don't want your toast cut in squares? Well, come on over here to the counter, and I'm going to teach you how to make your own toast. Then you can cut it whatever way you like!" From that day forward, she can be the official toast maker of the family.

SEEKING PROOF OF LOVE

1. What a child does:
   Interrupts parent when on the phone or chatting with a neighbor
   Shows off at school or is a clown at dinner
   Asks parent to do everything

2. How a parent reacts:
   Feels frustrated, annoyed, irritated, guilty
   Reminds, coaxes, does things the child can do for himself

3. Why a child acts this way:
   Seeking proof of love
   Believes Time = Love
   Thinks if the parent isn't attending to him, the parent is withdrawing love.

4. What you can do in situations like these:
   Show unconditional love
   Don't give attention when it's not appropriate
   Give attention when it is appropriate
   Take time for training
   Tell your child when you're going to be busy
   Do not do something a child can do for himself
   Plan special times
   Touch without words
   Say, for example, "I love you, and I will spend time with you when I'm off the phone"

2. SEEKING PROOF OF RESPECT

When children feel that they aren't being respected, they'll be hurt and discouraged, and they'll let us know. If we're lucky, they'll say, "Why do you get to decide all the time? That's not fair!" or, "It hurts my feelings when you yell at me."

We now have the opportunity to discuss the situation with the child and find a solution that feels respectful to both of us. The child no longer needs proof that he is, indeed, respected. This is when we feel terrific about our parenting.

If the child chooses not to share his thoughts with us, however, there's a good chance that he will seek respect by using power in one of two major ways. First, he will become angry and engage the parent in a power struggle with the goal of winning and getting his way. If this fails, his hurt feelings will escalate further, and he'll move into the second level of the power struggle because he feels justified in retaliating and seeking revenge. He'll "hurt out" because he feels hurt and misunderstood inside.

The power play

It's January, the snow is blowing, and it's time for school.

> *"Come on, hurry up!" you tell your nine-year-old. "Put your coat on, and get your hat and gloves."*
> *He doesn't move. "I don't want to wear my hat."*
> *"Well, that's too bad – it's cold out. Put it on."*
> *"No. It's a stupid hat."*
> *"It's not a stupid hat. It's nice and warm. Take it."*

The child takes it, looks at you in the eye, and says, "I'm going to drop it on the way to school."

This is a war of wills, and the nine-year-old boy is playing it with finesse. What he really wants here is respect, the recognition that he can decide for himself what he'll wear on a snowy January day. Yet by the time the power play flares up, it's easy to forget how the battle even began. When a dispute turns into a fight over power, we can usually tell by checking our own feelings. We might be angry or provoked by our child. We might think or say, "You'd better not, young man, or you'll be in trouble!" or, "I'll make you," or, "Why do you have to be so difficult all the time?" We might even feel threatened or defeated. It's tough, and most of us have been in this situation more than once in our parenting journey, maybe more than once a day.

Kids want respect from a very early age. Remember trying to put a diaper on a squirming infant? She can't talk yet, but she's trying to send us a message: "I'm the boss of my own body." It's the same story when you're wrestling with a toddler resisting that straightjacket we call a snowsuit or when you're fighting with your two-year-old over that chocolate chip cookie. The child wants a voice and a say over her life. She wants respect. You want to impose your will. The chocolate chip cookie is squished as the two of you lunge for it. Then she hits her pre-teens, and the topic of the power struggle switches to homework, screen time, and tattoos. Again, it's about respect. The child wants to decide how much screen time she has and when. You want to make that decision for her.

Our children can fight with us in an active way, by yelling, "You're not the boss of me!" or in a passive way, by dawdling. In this case, they're controlling us with their slowness. They can also ignore us, or give lip service to our demands, with no plan to follow through. They say, "Yeah, in a minute, Dad."

It's easy for parents to snap. After all, we have our eye on the needs of the situation and we don't believe our child does. The power struggle has now turned into a battle, and we're fighting our own child. We'd like our child to do what we say, but if he doesn't, what do we do? We pull out all the stops and use threats, bribes, and the guilt trip. But even these tactics can fail.

Kids can be incredibly persistent, especially when it comes to resisting what their parents want. The fact is that we can't force a child to get dressed, do her homework, or clean up her room, and she knows it. So some parents end up on a note of resignation, saying, "Do what you want. I am too tired to fight with you."

In our classes, we ask parents to act out a power struggle, and this is usually when they pump up the volume. One group of parents plays the children, and the other parents play themselves. They can choose any power play they like: Go to bed. Eat your dinner. Turn off the TV. Make your bed. Get dressed. Do your homework.

After one minute of shouting, we ask both groups how they feel. Parents say they feel provoked, angry, trapped, disrespected, exhausted. All felt powerless. Some think, *Are there any other parents with kids as bad as these?* Most parents can even feel the adrenaline surging through their body.

The children have some interesting comments, too. "No one listens to me. No one cares about me. I don't feel respected. It's my bed, why should you care if it's made. Close the door if you don't like looking at it. It's my life, so I should have a voice and say." And they think, *No matter what, I'm going to get my way. I'm not giving in to you.*

It's important to remember how power struggles start. They start with the child's desire for respect. If we're in a power struggle, it's likely that the child has bought into the idea that the person with the power gets the respect. It's usually driven by one of two beliefs: "I am powerful when I'm the boss," or, "I am powerful when I'm proving no one can boss me around."

Power struggles are children's way of saying that they aren't being respected, that they aren't being heard. What they're really saying is: "Listen to me. Give me choices. Let me express my ideas."

Meanwhile, the parent is thinking, *If he's being this difficult at age eight, what's he going to do at fifteen? Better to impose the rules now*, or, *It's important that kids listen to adults, just like I did.* We want our children to be successful in life, and we think we're imposing rules for their own good.

A power struggle can take on a life of its own. Once kids are in a power struggle, they don't want to submit. It would undermine their creative spirit and put them in an inferior, powerless position. They'd be losers. If they believe there are only two positions – powerful or powerless – children will go for power every time. So they start saying things that could be funny if they weren't so sad: "You're the worst dad ever!" "You can't play with my truck!" "You can't come to my birthday party!" "A grapefruit would be a better mother than you are!" Defiance enhances their sense of power. If the parent either gives in or gives up, they are the winner. Children feel like they've won even if they don't get what they want but do manage to drive their parent crazy.

A power struggle is detrimental to close relationships, even for the supposed winner. People who use power like this think it will force others to admire and respect them. Unfortunately, they get the opposite result. They actually distance themselves from other people. Nobody likes to be forced to do something, even if it's something they desire. Then, when using power does not give them what they really want, they escalate the power play and the cycle continues.

So what is a parent to do? It takes two to be in a power struggle, and we can control our own reactions even if we can't control our child's. So we need to remind ourselves, "I'm in charge of how I feel and what I do, not my child."

We need to recognize that we're in a power struggle and this struggle will hurt both us and our kids. One of us will win and the other will lose. The price of victory is high – distance from the person we love.

Power struggles take their toll. Instead of getting to school on time and feeling happy and ready to learn, kids start the day stressed and rushed. Instead of enjoying stories and cuddles with a parent before bed, kids fight with their parents about TV and about brushing their teeth. They get out of bed multiple times, until we snap at them.

So, when you find yourself in a power struggle, here are some effective solutions:

Disengage and withdraw.

If you've gotten yourself into a shouting match, take a deep breath, disengage, leave, and calm down. This is your time out. You probably need it. This is when you say, "I love you too much to fight. I am going upstairs until we are both calm," or, "You know what? Dad doesn't want to do this anymore. I'm taking a time out for me."

Yes. You go upstairs to your room, or you lock yourself in the bathroom if your child storms up the stairs behind you. This is counterintuitive to most of us. We believe the child should be removed, not us. After all, he started it! But who do we control? We control only ourselves and no one else. We may be able to drag a three-year-old upstairs with ease, but how are we going to get an eight-year-old to comply? Besides, that's not a caring way to treat a loved one, and it's not respectful to either party. It certainly isn't sending the message, "We can work this out."

Embrace positive, helpful self-talk.

"I love my child, but I don't love what she is doing at the moment!"

"This, too, will pass. Just believe in him and have some faith."

"I can't force my child to do anything. I can only invite her to work with me."

Once you're calm, go back and say, "Let's try again." In doing this, you're modeling an effective approach to resolving the inevitable conflicts in life.

We need to remind ourselves that our child wants to do well and wants to feel close to us. He also wants to have some power and control over his life. It's a good sign that he's fighting you to get it! It shows that he has spunk and the confidence to make his own decisions. Children who have more power over themselves do better in life, because they get opportunities to develop life skills such as independence, resourcefulness, decision making, and problem solving. They will also be less likely to mindlessly follow their peers.

Wait for a calm time to resolve conflicts.

Conflicts are normal in relationships and families. Learning how to manage them is an important part of our kids' social development. The key to handling conflict successfully is to deal with it respectfully and lovingly so that it doesn't flare up into a

MAGIC BULLET
Handling Power Struggles

When you're handling a power struggle, keep these five points in mind:

1. Have love, respect, and belief - in yourself and your child.
2. Be calm, or disengage until you are.
3. Ask yourself, "How might I have contributed to this conflict?"
4. Consider the long-range impact of your actions.
5. Ask yourself, "Am I teaching important life skills?"

power struggle. We can tell ourselves, "This is a good time to model respect to my child."

The most effective problem solving happens when parent and child are both calm, not when they're angry and agitated. You might say, "This isn't working. I think we need a little time to calm down." Notice the *we* here – *we* need calming down, not *you* need calming down. This non-accusatory phrase helps to gain cooperation when you do sit down to address the conflict.

Some parents insist on having the last word. This doesn't help build cooperation. A better way is to engage in discussions, not arguments. We want our children to respect other points of view and to accept differences. So at times it's best if we back off, let go, and give our children the room they need to figure things out for themselves.

Stop bossing.

When you try to manage and direct a child, it can make him feel inadequate. It hurts his sense of being respected, of having some control over his own person.

Offer limited choices.

In most cases, your child is fighting you because she wants more of a say in her life. When she refuses to put on her gloves after you tell her to, she's sending you the message, "What do you think I am, stupid? I can figure it out for myself," or, "It just makes me want to do the opposite when you tell me what to do!" When your son ignores all your requests to get dressed for school, he's sending the message, "I'd rather be late for school than give you the pleasure of thinking you can control me." If this is the case, you can offer him limited choices. When you present a power hungry child with a choice, he feels good because he's making the decision – not you!

Choices for the younger child:
"Do you want to get your clothes on in your room, or bring them down to the kitchen?"
"Do you want to wear the red or blue shirt today?"
"It's going to be cold today. Do you want to wear your mitts or tuck them in your pack?"

Choices for the older child:
"I'm available now to help you practice your times tables, or you can do them on your own later."
"Do you want to have your screen time after school or after dinner?"
"I'm willing to pay for the fifty-dollar shoes or you can use twenty-five dollars from your allowance and get the more expensive shoes. It's your choice."

It's not wise to give choices you aren't willing to accept. Giving a choice is not a way to trick or manipulate a child into compliance. A good choice helps the child meet his need to have a say in his life, and it also meets the needs of that situation. It feels respectful. Offering limited, reasonable choices is a good option.

Let routine be the boss.

You might sit down with your children in a quiet time and plan a routine. Routines work best when:

- The child has a say.
- We are consistent.
- We let the child experience the results of their choices.

When you have an agreed-upon routine and it's not working, make sure you give information rather than orders. For example, say, "Breakfast is ready." Then be quiet; resist the urge to say, "... so hurry up and get dressed." Show some faith – she knows the routine. If nothing happens, then you can ask a question or offer a choice.

"What is it you need to do before breakfast?" or, "Is there anything you have left to do before you eat?" In other words, get the child to focus on the needs of the situation, and then let her tell herself what to do. The routine becomes the boss, not the parent.

Ask what or how, not why.

This tip is a gift from parenting expert and author Jane Nelsen. Asking why invites defensive behavior, often drawing a blank face from a child. "What have you got left to do before we leave?" is a much more useful question than "Why aren't you ready yet?" If we can be curious and non-judgmental, using what and how questions, we have a better chance of helping our child focus on what has to be done.

Let your child experience the natural outcome of his choice.

If you give your child a choice, let him experience the result of his choice, as long as it's not life-threatening. If you've had the chance to establish a routine in advance and your child has agreed to it, then he can handle the outcome if he doesn't follow through. That means that if your child agrees to get dressed before breakfast and he goofs around instead, he might leave for school on an empty stomach. Letting him experience the natural result of his decision is a powerful way to teach him to make good decisions.

Ask for help.

You can show your child that you see him as competent and capable. "What can you do to help us get dinner on the table?" You can offer your child a job. "Would you like to set the table or do the veggie platter?" When kids are given a chance to contribute, they feel valued and more positive about their role in the family. There will be no need for nasty behavior.

Avoid retaliating when your child escalates.

> *Your five-year-old pees on the floor in the middle of another temper tantrum.*
>
> *You have a hard time getting your four-year-old child out the door in the morning, and he squirms and struggles as you force him into his car seat. To get even, he kicks the back of your seat the entire way to school, ignoring all your threats to make him stop.*

You win the jackpot during a game of Junior Monopoly. Your first-born says you cheated and knocks the entire game all over the floor.

Your seven-year-old is acting up again at the dinner table and you finally snap and send him to his room. After a few minutes you feel guilty and go to check on him. You open his door and see that he has ripped down his curtains and emptied every drawer of clothes onto the floor.

It's family night, and your ten-year-old wants to go for a sleepover. You say no, explaining that it's important to the family she stays. She has a meltdown and refuses to come out of her room for the entire evening.

You take away your twelve-year-old's cell phone because she was texting while doing homework. She yells that she hates you and wishes she had never been born into this family.

We can tell we've hit this stage by checking our own emotional pulse. We feel a big hurt. We are in disbelief and we feel defeated or bankrupt. We might find it hard to believe that our children could lash out at us in this way: *How could you do this to me? What did I do to deserve this?* Or we decide, *I'm a failure as a parent.* We might even go to a dark place. *I just don't like my child. Is he a bad seed?*

When we're hurt, our reflex is to hurt back and get even, even if it's with our own children. So, we take away privileges. We cancel their play date or sleepover, take away their allowance, ground them for life. Or we play our trump card. The deepest way to hurt children is to deny them our love. So we act cool and distant, ignore their questions, act even more warmly toward their siblings. We are seeking revenge, whether we're aware of it or not, and being as hurtful to our children as they were to us.

What's going on? We know how we feel – hurt and disappointed. If our child says, "I hate you!" it can hurt us deep inside. We need to tune into those feelings, because they will tell us a lot about our child's behavior. Behavior has a purpose and if we are feeling hurt, that is clearly the goal of their behavior. But why would a child want to hurt us?

It started with the child wanting respect and launching a power play to get it. He lost. Now he's seeking revenge to get back at you. Have you ever noticed that when a child chooses his target, he has a very accurate aim? If a parent is neat, he'll trash a room or knock holes in the wall. If a parent values punctuality, he'll dawdle for so long the parent will be late. If a parent is tight with money, he'll grab twenty dollars from the wallet. If a parent dotes on a younger sister, he'll knock her over.

If you and your child are caught in the downward spiral into revenge, what do you do? Here are a few ways of getting through this difficult time:

1. Don't overreact. If your eight-year-old child says, "I hate you," don't take it personally. At a moment like this, it's important to remember that she needs you desperately. Inside that angry exterior is your sweet child looking for a way out. She probably feels isolated and alone. It's best not to overreact. Resist saying, "That's not a nice thing to say," or, "That hurt my feelings." Your child has known this is not a nice way to talk

since she was five years old. If that doesn't seem possible, close your mouth and leave the room, saying, "I'll be back in a second." When you're ready, say to your child: "I gather you're very upset. Would you like to talk about it? Would a hug help?" Here, you're acknowledging your child's pain. You're empathizing with her. The message she hears is, "I love and care about you. I realize that something's not right for you and that's why you're behaving this way. I want to understand. I have confidence that together we can figure this out." We are empathizing but not agreeing. We are not saying, "I approve of your misbehavior." We are saying, "Let's try again. We'll find a better way to deal with the problem."

This is LRB – love, respect and belief – in action.

2. Avoid punishment and retaliation. Punishment doesn't work in the long run. It will only escalate the battle and separate you emotionally from your child. Instead, the child has to be given a chance to contribute to the fix. Ask him, "What are we going to do about this?" Give him a chance to clean up if he made a mess or find some way to make it better if he hurt someone.

3. Build trust. At a moment like this, the child sees you as the enemy. She thinks you don't care about her and that you don't respect her. You need to show her that you do care, you do understand her point of view, and you want to respect her. Start by listening carefully to how she feels. Learn what her point of view is. Explain what you need. Then collaborate to figure out how you are going to fix the immediate problem and deal with the deeper issue that led to this struggle.

SEEKING PROOF OF RESPECT

1. What a child does:
   Disobeys the rules
   Shows defiance: "You're not the boss of me! You can't make me!"
   Dawdles and ignores the needs of the situation
   Punches a sibling

2. How the parent reacts:
   Feels provoked, challenged, threatened, defeated
   Thinks, "You can't get away with this!"
   Says, "You will do it because I said so!"

3. Why the child does this:
   Wants proof of respect
   Wants more power and control over his body and life
   Thinks, "I can do this for myself and my parent won't let me"
   Wants to get even for injustices
   Thinks, "She or he is so unfair"
   Thinks, "Nobody cares or understands me"

4. What the parent can do:
   Show respect for the child
   Stop controlling and managing
   Withdraw, disengage, and cool off
   Offer choices whenever possible
   Let routine be the boss - not the parent
   Let the child experience outcome of her choices

If child is in revenge mode:
- Avoid punishment or retaliation
- Listen carefully to child's feelings and point of view
- Build trust in the relationship
- Help child to make amends
- Don't take his behavior personally

3. SEEKING PROOF OF BELIEF

Every once in a while, we see a child who has given up on himself. This is a child who has lost all self-confidence and may think his parent does not value or believe in him. He's so hurt that he generally doesn't say anything at all. He may just retreat into his room and give up on trying anything. Or he may push his parent away and disconnect emotionally.

It happened to a boy we know in grade three. He loved school and learning until a perfectionist of a teacher came along. She'd tear up work in front of the children and tell them to do it over because it wasn't good enough. The little boy retreated into his shell. At home, he played in his room more; he didn't want to go on play dates. The teacher had squeezed the confidence out of him.

When a child is unsure about his ability to handle the challenges and hurts of day-to-day life, he can give up and lose hope. A child like this becomes passive, unwilling to make even the smallest effort for fear that he will not be good enough or be criticized. This passivity is a bad sign. He might be thinking, *I am hopeless and unable to do this,* or *It's no use trying because I won't do it right.* He's saying, "I can't do it. I'm unable to handle the potential disappointment, embarrassment, and hurt of failure, so I will convince others not to expect anything of me."

What can a parent do? Here, the challenge is to instill confidence in the disheartened child. It takes time, and it's important to take little steps to do it.

- Refrain from criticism. Reinforce his value and importance to the family.
- Encourage any positive attempt. Break tasks down into small steps, and teach the skills, or show how – but don't do it for him.
- Express your faith in your child's ability to learn. Focus on his strengths rather than pointing out his weaknesses.
- The more power you can give your child in a situation like this, the better. Let him decide what to have for breakfast and what to wear. Let him have as much control as you can give him without affecting you or the rest of your family in a negative way.
- And, most importantly, don't give up! With determination and your unshakeable love for your child, this, too, will pass.

SEEKING PROOF OF BELIEF

1. What the child does:
   Withdraws from parent, or life, both physically and emotionally
   Goes into his shell
   Won't try anything
2. How the parent reacts:
   Feels lost and helpless
   Pushes the child harder or gives up on her
   Does everything for the child
3. Why a child does this:
   Feels deeply hurt, hopeless, and unworthy
   Has no faith or confidence in himself
   May think parent doesn't believe in him
   Has been criticized too much
   Has been humiliated over mistakes or inadequacies
4. What the parent should do:
   Show belief in child's ability to learn
   Stop all criticism
   Reinforce her value and importance to the family
   Be patient; take it step by step
   Celebrate small successes
   Don't do things the child can do herself
   Encourage, encourage, encourage

EXERCISE: DETERMINING YOUR CHILD'S GOALS

Record a recent struggle you had with one of your children (argument, act of defiance, temper tantrum, dawdling).

1. Background:
   a. Describe the situation you and your child were in.

   b. Describe the details of the conflict:

      - Recall your words and actions (e.g., I turned the TV off and said, "Go upstairs and get ready for bed").

      - Recall your child's reaction (include his words and actions).

      - What thoughts did you have? (e.g., *Here we go again ...*).

2. How did the behavior make you feel?

What did you do then?

3. What was your child's reaction to your response?

Put yourself in your child's shoes for the moment ...
How might your child have interpreted your response?

4. Checking the chart, what might your child be seeking? Your love, respect, or belief in them?

5. What might be a more helpful way to approach the situation should it happen again?

Acknowledgement: Beverley Cathcart-Ross, Saskatoon Adlerian Society

SEEKING PROOF AT A GLANCE

Seeking Proof of Love

1. What a child does:
   Interrupts parent on the phone or when chatting with a neighbor
   Shows off at school or is a clown at dinner
   Asks parent to do everything

2. How a parent reacts:
   Feels frustrated, annoyed, irritated, guilty
   Parent reminds, coaxes, does things the child can do for himself

3. Why a child acts this way:
   Seeking proof of love
   Believes Time = Love
   Thinks if the parent isn't attending to him all the time, parent is withdrawing love.

4. What you can do in situations like these:
   Show unconditional love
   Don't give attention when it's not appropriate
   Give attention when it is appropriate
   Take time for training
   Preview, give child information before you are going to be busy
   Do not do something a child can do for himself
   Plan special times
   Touch without words
   Say something like, "I love you and I will spend time with you when I'm off the phone"

Seeking Proof of Respect

1. What a child does:
   - Disobeys the rules
   - Is defiant: "You're not the boss of me!" "You can't make me!"
   - Dawdles and ignores the needs of the situation
   - Punches a sibling

2. How the parent reacts:
   - Feels provoked, challenged, threatened, defeated
   - Thinks, "You can't get away with this!"
   - Says, "You will do it because I said so!"

3. Why the child does this:
   - Wants proof of respect
   - Wants more power and control over his body and life
   - Thinks, "I can do this for myself and my parent won't let me"
   - Wants to get even for injustices
   - Thinks, "She or he is so unfair"
   - Thinks, "Nobody cares about me or understands me"

4. What the parent can do:
   - Show respect for the child
   - Stop controlling and managing
   - Withdraw, disengage, and cool off
   - Offer choices wherever possible
   - Let routine be the boss – not the parent
   - Let child experience outcome of choices

If child is in revenge mode:
   - Avoid punishment or retaliation
   - Listen carefully to child's feelings and point of view

Build trust in the relationship
Help child to make amends
Don't take his behavior personally

Seeking Proof of Belief

1. What the child does:
   Withdraws from the parent, or life, both physically and emotionally
   Goes into his shell
   Won't try anything

2. How the parent reacts:
   Feels lost and helpless
   Pushes the child harder or gives up on child
   Does everything for the child

3. Why a child does this:
   Feels deeply hurt, hopeless, and perhaps not worthy
   Has no faith or confidence in himself
   May think parent doesn't believe in him
   Has been criticized too much
   Has been humiliated over mistakes or inadequacies

4. What the parent should do:
   Show belief in child's ability to learn
   Stop all criticism
   Reinforce her value and importance to the family
   Be patient: take it step by step
   Celebrate small successes
   Don't do things the child can do herself
   Encourage, encourage, encourage

6

Stop Flogging a Dead Horse: Why Punishment Is Self-Defeating

Were you punished as a child? How? We like to give parents in our classes the opportunity to discuss this sensitive topic. The answers they give us are painfully illuminating.

> *"I was spanked with a wooden spoon, and I still have it. I don't cook with it, though."*
>
> *"I was spanked with a feather duster. I didn't know, for a long time, that it was actually designed to clean the house."*
>
> *"I was made to feel guilty and ashamed."*
>
> *"I had my privileges and allowance taken away for stupid reasons."*
>
> *"I was grounded and I wasn't allowed to see my friends for two whole weeks."*
>
> *"I was spanked with a hairbrush."*
>
> *"I was spanked with a belt."*
>
> *"I was locked in my room."*

"I had to get on my knees in the corner."

"My mother washed out my mouth with soap."

DOES PUNISHMENT WORK?

The purpose of this punishment was presumably to make the child pay for what she had done. Or perhaps it was to teach the child a lesson. Did that work? We asked parents how they felt as children when they were punished this way. They said they felt ashamed, angry, fearful, humiliated, powerless. Some people hated their parents. They felt hurt, confused. They felt it was unfair and disrespectful. They felt misunderstood, not cared for. Some people vowed not to get caught next time. Some were vengeful. It's very rare to hear a parent say, "I deserved it."

Some parents do say it worked. They didn't act out again. "If it worked for me, then why shouldn't it work for my child today?" they ask. To those parents we say, yes, it's important that children are held accountable for their behavior, but this does not have to be done in a hurtful way. Children do not have to suffer at the hands of their parents to learn. It might be helpful to remember our misbehaving child is discouraged or hurt about something. She probably wants to be reassured of our love, or perhaps she wants us to respect her right to decide, or she may even be feeling misunderstood and alone. She's trying to tell us something.

"I'm old enough to be in charge of my homework."

"Why do I need to have a bath every night?"

"Why do you always take his side?"

So how will she feel if we punish her? She won't feel better. If she's already discouraged, she'll be made to feel a lot worse. We are even validating her mistaken idea that we don't care or understand. And we certainly won't be addressing the reason our child misbehaved in the first place or preventing it from happening again!

THE NEED TO PUNISH

Still, many of us feel we need to punish our children when they do something wrong. Most of us today won't use physical punishment, but we can hurt our children with emotional punishments – the most powerful being the withdrawal of our love and closeness. Or, we can restrict their natural desire to create and explore by removing privileges. We can make them sit still or on a naughty mat to "think about it," for example. We can cancel hockey practice or a trip to the park where they can burn off excess energy. We can prevent them from attending a birthday party where they enjoy social interaction. We can separate siblings instead of teaching conflict resolution skills.

When we do this, we often make things worse. Sure, punishment can work in the short term for some children. It may stop the bad behavior, if only because we instill fear in our kids with the message, "If you do this, something bad will happen to you." But it won't work for long. Our child will go underground and continue her behavior in a covert or sneaky way, trying to get away with it. Or, she might ramp it up and try to punish us back. The struggle has now become the focus of our relationship with our child, instead of the practical issue (such as nutrition, cleanliness, school work, or staying safe) that set off the dispute.

MAGIC BULLET
A Memorandum from a Child

Don't be inconsistent. That confuses me and makes me try harder to get away with everything that I can.

Don't make me feel smaller than I am. I will make up for it by behaving like a "big shot."

Don't try to discuss my behavior in the heat of a conflict. For some reason my hearing is not very good at this time and my cooperation is even worse.

Don't try to preach to me. You'd be surprised how well I know what's right and wrong.

Don't protect me from the result of my choices. I need to learn from experience.

Don't forget to apologize if you are wrong. An honest apology makes me feel better and shows you care about my feelings. It will help me feel safe to apologize, too.

–Anonymous

AN EXTERNAL MOTIVATOR

What do we mean by *punishment*, anyway? The Merriam-Webster dictionary defines it this way: "Suffering, pain or loss that serves as retribution." To qualify as a punishment, suffering must occur – physical, mental or emotional suffering. The dictionary goes on to give us an example: "I took away my daughter's car keys as punishment for a bad behavior." Punishment is an external motivator. The message is that we have no belief that the child can learn unless we remove a privilege or hurt them in some way. This shows a loss of faith in our guiding principle and attitude – Love, Respect and Belief. Dr. Nash calls this "falling flat in our faith."

When we checked other parenting books on this topic, every single author we could find warned that punishing children produces detrimental effects.

- Dr. Haim Ginott, in his book *Between Parent and Child* ... "Punishment is worse than useless [...] It only results in a charged atmosphere, an irritated parent and an angry child."
- Dr. Rudolf Dreikurs, in *Children: The Challenge* ... "We live in an age of increasing democratization, where we no longer rely on authorities to tell us what to do and to make us 'toe the line.' "
- Adele Faber, in *How to Talk So Kids Will Listen and Listen so Kids Will Talk* ... "Punishment is a distraction.

> Instead of the child feeling sorry for what he has done and thinking about how he can make amends, he becomes preoccupied with revenge fantasies."

CONSEQUENCES: PUNISHMENTS IN DISGUISE

Parents are becoming more and more comfortable with the idea of consequences. Punishment isn't appropriate in today's society, so with good intentions we choose to use "consequences" instead. However, most of us do not implement consequences effectively. Our consequences are usually just punishments in disguise.

In addition, most parents tell us that logic flies out the window at times, especially when their child is challenging them. That's when that urge to cause some damage can surface. They find that the reflex to get back at their children, get even with them, or make them pay for their behavior kicks in and is difficult to ignore.

So why do we punish? There are many reasons. Perhaps we don't know what else to do; we feel bankrupt. Or, we need to relieve the frustration building up when we confront a child who won't bend to our will. We might even feel a fleeting sense of satisfaction when we punish, because we feel that at least we've done something in a difficult situation. Many parents punish because they feel the pressure of judgment from another parent or adult. They don't want to lose the approval of others.

PUNISHMENT AND FEAR

On a deeper level, we punish because of an ancient instinct similar to those we talked about in chapter four. Our colleague Dr. Nash sums it up like this: "Parents punish out of love and caring. Parents instinctually want safety and survival for their children. Survival used to be in question on a daily basis. Families faced dictators and plagues and spent all of their time and energy meeting basic needs like shelter and food. The best shot at survival was to avoid risk, be obedient and submissive to those in power." If a child made a mistake, it could have been fatal, and the parents knew it.

Today, you can be pretty sure your child will rebel if you try to order him around or punish him if he doesn't toe the line. The reason for this is not biological, but social. When parents bossed their children around as a normal course of action, they were living in societies that were organized along hierarchical lines. In business, the boss was king; you couldn't challenge him if you wanted to keep your job. The same was true in other social organizations, including the family. (Substitute father or mother for king.) But now, in the twenty-first century, things have changed. The power structure in society is no longer top to bottom but more horizontal. If you have ever gotten a second medical opinion, switched lawyers, questioned a religious practice, or been grateful that schools no longer have the right to spank your children, you know this new structure makes sense.

When parents and children have equal rights to human dignity and respect, punishment is inappropriate. It puts parents in a position of superiority and children in a position of inferiority. In other words, when your child says, "You're not the boss of me," it's surprising to many of us to realize that he has a very good point.

THE PRICE OF PUNISHMENT

Let's look at the issue from another perspective. What is the price we pay, as parents, when we punish our child?

- The child resists, becomes defiant, or rebels.
- Even worse, the child may withdraw and become passive or feel rejected.
- Parents model poor behavior, and their child will most likely copy them when they get angry – with the parent, with a friend, or eventually with their own children.
- Parents teach their child to obey and be afraid – definitely not the life skills most parents have in mind for the long term.
- More importantly, punishment can push the child away from his parent and, in extreme cases, it may even distort his understanding of love and respect. He may equate love with fear, and respect with dominance of others, which will lead to plenty of trouble in years ahead.

What do we need to do as parents when we feel the urge to punish or lash out after our child has made a mistake or is not doing what he's told?

- Recognize how powerful the reflex to control and punish is, and where it comes from – an ancient need to protect our kids.
- Thank these reflexes; they keep us alive.
- Ask, "Is this a life or death situation?"
- If it's not life-threatening, step back and give the child room to make a choice.
- If his choice doesn't work out well, don't protect him from the outcome of his judgment. Let him know that you have confidence in his ability to handle it and you are there for him if he needs you, as a safety net.

It may be tempting to punish your eleven-year-old child who doesn't do his homework. Pulling screen time may be a very attractive option. What should we do? We care about his success in school and worry that if we don't interfere, his marks will slip.

The first step is to remind ourselves that this isn't a life or death situation. Furthermore, what's at stake here is bigger than a book report. This is about our child developing the skills to assess and manage his responsibilities. Our role is now consultant; we are a resource for him.

We also need to show our child that we have confidence in his ability to figure this out for himself. If he uses poor judgment, the outcome will be his to handle. Perhaps he'll need to stay up late to make up for that extra screen time he took. Perhaps the teacher will keep him in at recess to finish his report. He may even surprise us and ask for our help to better organize his time.

Either way, he is learning that the buck starts and stops with him. We need to respect his right to make that choice for himself. Yes, it can be uncomfortable for us to watch in the short term, but the payoff of letting him gain experience is huge in the long term.

What about the child who grabs a couple of chocolate chip cookies five minutes before dinner? Many of us have been in this situation, and we might get really annoyed about the cookie grab. After all, she knows the deal – no cookies before supper! What can we do? Again, remember, this isn't life or death. Also remember where this anger comes from: We're concerned our child will not eat supper or get proper nourishment, so we react. When she doesn't show respect for the situation, we feel we must make her comply or experience a consequence.

RESISTING THE URGE TO PUNISH

If our child doesn't comply with family agreements, we should resist that reflexive urge to make him pay for it. Instead, we might choose to ask him:

> *"When do we have cookies in our house?"*
> *Or, "If you want cookies, how about you put some on a plate for dessert and we can all enjoy them."*
> *Or, "I'm upset you are not respecting our deal of 'no cookies before dinner.' I think we'd better talk about this later, when we're both calm."*

And make sure you do follow through. Self-talk helps:

"I will do my best to guide my children."
"I will be caring and accepting of myself even when things don't work out."
"My worthiness is not in question."
"I will handle the outcome and learn better for the next time."

A CASE IN POINT: ACTING ON THE PRINCIPLE OF DUAL RESPECT

A Letter from a Frustrated Parent

Dear Martin and Georgine,

I would like your advice on a constantly recurring problem I have with my seven-year-old son. Most of the time he is quite reasonable and helpful, caring toward his little sister, and generally pleasant to be with.

However, he doesn't want to listen when I tell him to do or not to do certain things. For example, I specifically told him not to eat candy just before dinner. He looked at me and stuffed the candy right into his mouth. What should I do? How should I punish him for not listening to me?

–Frustrated Parent

Dear Frustrated Parent,

Your question is a common one; all parents have struggled with this issue. When you say "he doesn't listen to me," what you actually mean is "he does not obey me."

He can hear you all right, so he is listening; however, he does not comply with your wishes.

We know that you want to be a responsible parent and are concerned for his nutritional needs as well as his growth and development, but punishing him for disobedience is not an effective way to convey this concern.

Punishment is inappropriate in our democratic society, in which both parents and children have equal rights to human dignity and respect. It puts the parent in a position of superiority and the child in a position of inferiority.

Punishment by its definition has to hurt, and it will likely bring on the negative effects of the use of power. It can nurture resentment, retaliation, and rebellion, or it can drive his behavior underground (i.e., he will continue his behavior in a sneaky way and will try to get away with it). Your focus is then on the power struggle and who will win it, rather than meeting the needs of the situation, looking after our nutrition and respecting our bodies.

Rebellious behavior is often a payback for injustices and grievances suffered in the past. When we use our power over our child, even if we win a round, he will just bide his time to get back at us on the next occasion he can show us the "you can't make me" attitude.

There are children who will submit to our demands - but is this in their best interest? If they submit to us, they may also be quick to submit to the demands of their peers and to become "pleasers" in life instead of independent, self-motivated individuals.

Sometimes it may seem that punishment has worked for the moment, but the damage to your relationship is accumulating.

If our goal becomes to not resort to punishment or other disrespectful approaches to conflicts, how can we handle these frustrating moments? Instead of getting angry and resorting to the use of power, you could do the following:

Give your son information; share with him why you don't want him to have the candy right now.

Ask for his ideas on how this situation could be handled (when is candy a good idea, when do we have candy in our house, etc.).

Find solutions for the next time. If the candy has already been eaten, you may want to talk about what you can agree on for the future.

Implement consequences - What is the "Logical Next Step?" If your child continues to show no regard for his candy consumption and therefore his health, you may decide there might not be candy in the house until he is willing to be more respectful of the situation and your agreements.

We don't want to live in a war zone with our children. We want to have closeness and dual respect, where we respect their right to make judgments but do not lose sight of our own self-respect. For example, our child "forgets" to take his lunch to school. We can respect his decision to do this and have faith that he will handle the outcome of his action. Out of self-respect, we don't make the extra trip to deliver his lunch to the school.

When a behavior is questionable, we should see what the needs of the situation dictate, rather than trying to make the child do something because we dictate it. When in doubt about how to handle an issue, explore what would be mutually respectful through problem solving, and together agree on a solution that you both can live with.

Yours truly,

Martin and Georgine

EXERCISE: THE LOGICAL NEXT STEP

When tempted to use punishment, try using the tool of the Logical Next Step instead. This requires letting go of fear when our child makes a mistake and accepting that mistakes can be great opportunities for you both to learn.

Here's an example, adapted from the work of Adele Faber and Elaine Mazlish, of a how a dad deals with his frustration effectively when his son is not showing respect for his leather catcher's mitt. Practice this approach on the next problem you may have with a child.

1. Express your feelings without attacking your child or their character. (Focus on the action, not the child.)

   "I'm upset that my mitt was left outside in the dirt and rain. The leather will get dry and cracked."

2. Share how you want your property to be treated.

   "I want my things to be returned in good condition after you use them."

3. Ask the child how he can correct the problem. If he doesn't know, show him.

   "What this mitt needs now is to be carefully dried and treated with some petroleum jelly."

4. Ask your child for a plan going forward or give him a choice.

   "You can borrow my mitt and put it away properly, or you can give up the privilege of using it. You decide."

5. Acknowledge any effort to improve.

   "I noticed my mitt is being put away these days. Thanks for your cooperation."

6. If the problem persists, follow through or take action.

   Child: "Dad, I can't find your baseball mitt."
   Father: "For the time being, I have put it away. I want to know my mitt is in the condition I left it. When you are ready to take more care you can borrow it again."

7. Problem-solve. Explore ways to improve the situation with your child.

   "What can we work out so that you can use my mitt when you play catch, and I can be assured it will be treated with respect?"

"Give It Your Best Shot": How Encouragement Strengthens Self-Esteem

Children, as we've seen, may act up if they feel discouraged, hurt, or excluded from a group. Sometimes the problem is that they hurt inside; they feel badly about themselves. We can think of this as a problem of self-esteem. When we use this word, many parents think it means having a big dose of confidence or thinking you can conquer the world. But this is not what we mean.

WHAT SELF-ESTEEM REALLY MEANS

Self-esteem means "how I estimate myself." Our perception of ourselves depends on how we feel about ourselves or what we believe to be true about ourselves. How other people think we should feel about ourselves doesn't really matter. You could be the most beautiful girl on the block but feel like an ugly duckling. As an adult, you might look totally in control and calm in the middle of chaos, but be riddled with self-doubt and anxiety.

How does this happen? Children are born with their self-esteem intact. We have never met a baby who apologizes for his flaws:

"Sorry about the nose, it's a little big."
"My hair will grow in soon, I promise."
"Sorry about that smelly diaper."

No, they lie on that change table looking happy. They are fully accepting of themselves. That's what it looks like to be free of self-criticism and negative self-talk.

HOW CHILDREN LOSE THEIR SELF-ESTEEM

If we are born with our esteem intact, why does it become such an issue?

Why do we have children chewing their nails to the quick, not wanting to go to school, afraid of trying, afraid of mistakes? An increasing number of kids with anxiety or stress or who think they are not good enough? No wonder parents are so afraid.

What happens? Their world (mom, dad, siblings, relatives, peers, teachers) starts giving them feedback:

"He's so stubborn. He was like that from the day he was born."
"She is such an angel – sleeps right through the night."
"It's too bad he got my nose."
"What a monkey! She wants to climb everything. She's the opposite of her brother."

We all do it. Unfortunately, the kids are listening! Over time they don't feel as perfect; they might even start feeling they're not lovable or capable, even though that wasn't our intention at all. They also learn that their performance is being measured, and it doesn't take long for them to connect their performance to their worth.

WHEN ENCOURAGEMENT = DISCOURAGEMENT

But there is good news here. We have tremendous influence over how children perceive themselves. If we can hurt a child's self-esteem, we can help it, too.

Our first priority is to be clear on whether we are being encouraging or discouraging.

We often tell our children how much we think they can do it, but this can put pressure on them to be successful right away, and it may not be effective. Do you ever wonder why your child doesn't believe you when you say, "I know you'll be great at it"? The one acting in this sentence is the parent, not the child. The child hears that the parent knows, but it doesn't give the child herself any confidence.

An encouraging parent, on the other hand, wants to help the child believe she can handle it. With this idea in mind, we coined the term *enhandlement*. You may recall that enhandlement means "reinforcing children's belief in their ability to handle a situation" and it places the focus on children's need to believe in their ability to handle what comes their way.

We've all watched our children try to tie their shoelaces.

It takes time for a child's brain and fingers to figure it out, and a lot of times, to be helpful, we'll do it for our child or we'll say:

"Let Mommy do it, it will be faster."

This is a discouraging remark. It's better to say:

"You're really working hard here. One day your fingers will figure this out. Do you want to practice a little more, or do you want Mommy to give you a hand?"
Or, "I know you want to do some more practicing, but we've run out of time. Why don't we practice when we get home from school?"

If encouragement, or enhandlement, inspires belief and confidence in one's ability, discouragement takes belief and confidence away. It can make a child feel he can't do it or think, *What's the point? I can never please her.* It can happen when parents try to manage and control their child or when they point out what's not working. We say things like, "Why are you always late?" "Why can't you be more organized?" "You haven't even put your backpack together! What's the matter with you?" These comments, aimed to correct and improve, can really discourage a child. By the end of the day, he might feel that there's nothing positive about himself.

Of course this discouragement is not what we intend. We think that by pointing out shortcomings, we protect the child from struggling or experiencing failure. Sometimes, we are

MAGIC BULLET
How We May Unknowingly Hurt with Our Words

Instead of saying:

"Here, let me tie your laces for you. We're in a hurry."

Be encouraging; focus on learning and improvement:

"Look at that! You're learning to tie your own shoe laces."

Or, "It's time for us to leave. Would you like to finish those laces in the car, or shall I give you a bit of help this time?"

Instead of saying:

"I saw some errors on your project after you went to bed last night. I hope you don't mind that I corrected them for you. It looks much better now."

Be encouraging; focus on effort:

"I read your project last night. I never knew that was why a snake shed its skin. You've certainly done your research."

Instead of saying:

"No, honey, I'd prefer to sweep the floor myself. Getting the dirt out of those corners can be tricky, you know!"

Be encouraging; show appreciation:

"Thank you! The kitchen floor is much cleaner now.

Do you want to see a trick I use to get the dirt out of those corners?"

Instead of saying:

"I don't want you wearing that shirt - it's all wrinkled. What's Grandma going to think if you turn up looking like that?"

Be encouraging; respect the child's choice:

"You know, Grandma's pretty fussy about how we dress for her Sunday dinner. If you'd really like to wear that shirt, what do you think about taking an iron to it?"

critical with the intention of motivating better performance, a form of reverse psychology. However, the result is often the opposite of what we hope.

What does discouragement sound like? We went to the school yard one day to find out. We asked some children, ages five to fourteen, a simple question: "What do your parents do that you find discouraging?"

> *"They're always telling me or reminding me of things that I already know, like don't swing too high on the swings, or don't play too close to the road."*
> *"I'm fourteen and my parents still treat me like I'm a kid. It makes me feel like I can't accomplish anything."*

"My parents don't really listen when I ask for a later bedtime. I'm eight and going to bed at the same time as my little sister."

"I can't really do anything. My dad wants to know where I am all the time. My curfew is nine still, even on Friday and Saturday."

"I think my mom doesn't want to let me go and that's 'cause I'm her last kid."

"My dad, he yells louder than two police sirens as if the police put his voice for a siren. It would be two times louder than that whenever he is really, really in a bad temper."

"They won't let me get my driver's license either, even though I have my beginner's permit. I had to get it myself, behind their back."

Compare these young voices with your own memories of someone from your childhood who encouraged you, believed in you, and helped you feel good about yourself. We asked our parents to share their memories:

"A lady who lived down the street from me made me feel special, and because I was from a large family it was nice to have that alone time with somebody who took an interest in me."

"This uncle was a marvelous old guy. I felt I was his able assistant, that I could make a contribution. If I made a mistake, he never passed judgment; he never scolded me or said anything negative. He was always so calm."

"She taught me to walk my own road and listen to my own music, regardless of what anybody else said."

An encourager shows a child that she is valued and loved, no matter what. She is valued for her own individuality and creativity – not what her parent wants her to be. Encouragers emphasize the love of learning and exploring, not the fear of failure. Encouragers also do certain things. Here are a few key practices:

TEN ENCOURAGEMENT PRACTICES

1. MAKE TIME FOR YOUR CHILDREN

No matter how busy you are, set aside some moments in the day when you can focus on them and listen to them. This is when you can be physically, mentally, and emotionally available to your child. Say you're cooking dinner and your child comes into the kitchen looking sullen. He wants to tell you about a big problem at school. While you can do your best to listen, he won't feel he has your undivided attention while you're cooking. So you can say:

> *"This sounds very important to you, and I want to hear every word. So give me five minutes to get this in the oven, and then I can be all yours."*

The message your child gets is that you care, he's important, and his feelings are valued in this family.

Your child climbs into the car and tries to show you her artwork in the back seat while you're driving. You can say this:

"You know what, I would love to see the art you did today, and when we get home I want to sit down and have you show me what you've been working on."

She may be frustrated at having to wait, but the experience in the end will be much more valuable to her. You can even book dates with your kids. Have one-on-one time with each child. It's special for you and it's special for them.

2. TREAT MISTAKES AS AN OPPORTUNITY TO LEARN

They're positive and they're human. They're a sign that your child is exploring her world and is willing to take some risks. So, when mistakes happen, say:

"Okay, a mistake happened. What can we learn from this? What would you do next time?"

For example, your five-year-old child was being a little rambunctious at the table and knocks over a glass of water. It falls onto the floor and breaks. You say:

"You have a bit of a mess here, don't you? How about I show you how to clean this up safely."

You grab some cloths from under the sink.

"We'll mop it up, but we have to be very careful 'cause there's broken glass here. Maybe we had better get the dog out of the room first. We wouldn't want him to hurt his paws."

We can take that moment and make it an opportunity for the child to learn, realize that he is accountable for his actions, and see that he can handle cleanups.

3. LIGHTEN UP WITH HUMOR

Humor puts everything into perspective. It gives us a break from our too-serious lives. Look for ways to inject it into your family life.

We know one family with a three-year-old daughter who was very prone to temper tantrums. One night, her dad approached his wife minutes before dinner and said he wanted a chocolate chip cookie.

His wife looked at him and said, "We don't have chocolate chip cookies before dinner, Dan, you know that."

At that, the dad threw his six-foot body on the floor and started kicking and wailing. His three-year-old daughter was standing there, wide-eyed, watching his performance. At the end, all three, daughter included, had a good laugh over silly daddy.

He swears that turned her off temper tantrums.

4. FOCUS ON EFFORT AND IMPROVEMENT

You can start simply by describing what you see happening, what you notice:

"I noticed you helping ... I noticed how hard you've been working, I noticed how this new book really interests you ..."

Your child comes down the stairs and he has completely dressed himself for the first time. You can say:

"Wow, I see you've put your shirt on and your pants on and you've done it all by yourself."

It's much better than "What a good boy." Show your children you're noticing their efforts, their improvement, and the things they have accomplished. When your child is struggling with multiplication, you can say:

"You know what; you've come a long way. I remember when you struggled with subtraction, and it's a breeze for you now. The multiplication will come, too."

Let them see some history:

"I remember when you couldn't even put your socks on and now you're doing up your shoes."

This lets the child see that progress happens and effort counts. Focus on how they're contributing and on how their actions make a difference. For example, you can say:

"Thank you for bringing your dishes to the counter. Cleanup is going to go much faster now, don't you think?"

5. TURN LIABILITIES INTO ASSETS

As a parent, you can always turn a liability into an asset. Take a child you think is bossy and stubborn. See the silver lining. With time and guidance, bossy can become a good leader, and stubborn can become determined and tenacious. These are characteristics we actually admire in other adults. Instead of saying to your child, "Stop being bossy to your brother," you could say:

"It sounds like you have a lot of good ideas, but your brother just isn't willing to listen right now."

To your determined child you could say:

"You really want to wear this dress to school today, don't you? Well, why don't we tuck a sweater into your backpack just in case you find it a little cool."

This way, you'll avoid getting into a power struggle, and you're reinforcing your belief in her ability to figure this out. This is enhandlement in action!

6. LISTEN

Be a pair of ears, empathetic and understanding, when your child is sharing a heartfelt story or a problem. It may be difficult for you at first, but don't deny their feelings or give advice.

7. SHOW APPRECIATION FOR WHAT THEY DO

Show appreciation for the little or big things they do.

> *"I appreciated your help today."*
> *"I appreciated your patience at the store."*
> *"It was thoughtful of you to help your brother with his boots."*

Let them know you appreciate their help around the house. When a child feels you've noticed, it encourages his efforts and gives him that good feeling associated with contributing and doing for others.

> *"Thanks for setting the table. Dinner is ready faster when we all contribute. Now you and I have more time for stories later."*

When you focus on the effort that they are making, they'll see they are valued and needed within the family. Let them overhear you bragging about them to another parent or to Grandma on the phone.

> *"Yesterday when I was sick, Jamie brought his book and sat and read me stories – it felt terrific."*

When your children hear you talk about them in these ways, they really do pat themselves on the back and say "Hey, yeah, I'm an okay guy." If you go out for dinner, treat your child as you would a friend. You would never tell a friend at the end of a meal, "You behaved really well today, and your manners were terrific!" So, if your family outing went well, you can say:

> *"I had a wonderful time tonight. Let's do this again."*

8. LOVE UNCONDITIONALLY

Let your child know that your love doesn't change because she is not performing well today. Kids under age five don't understand this easily. They think, *Mommy raised her voice at me. She doesn't love me right now*. So make sure to use love in your language with them.

> *"I love you too much to fight; I'm going to the other room right now until we're both calm."*
> *"You know I love you, but this isn't working for Mommy right now."*
> *"You're having a hard day, aren't you? Do you need a hug?"*

All these messages let your child know that your love is always there. It's not lost because she has done something that upset you.

Children expect us to love them at certain times – when they are going to sleep at night and when they are going off to school. They expect us to love them when they are doing well. They least expect us to love them when they are not doing well.

Keep that love shining through, especially when they don't expect it.

9. RESPECT YOURSELF AND YOUR CHILD

The long-term value of respecting your child's right to make judgments is that they develop self-confidence, a key element of self-esteem. They develop good judgment. They'll make a lot of mistakes along the way, but remember, that's okay. Mistakes are a sign of effort, of learning and growing. Let your child choose and experience the pleasure of overcoming struggles and the joy he'll get from his successes.

10. BELIEVE IN YOUR CHILD – PRACTICE ENHANDLEMENT

If you let a child go to school in a mismatched outfit, she may start a fashion trend – or she may struggle because someone teases her. As parents, it's our job to sit and listen, to help her sort through this and see that she can handle it and not stay hurt.

If your son didn't get that project done on time, he has to go to school and tell the teacher he didn't get his work done. It will probably be uncomfortable for him. You can let him know that you're there should he want your help, but the overriding message is, "This is yours to handle, and you will figure this out."

So, show confidence in your child's ability to learn.

"I believe you can handle this."
"I have seen you do things that are harder than this."
"I have confidence you can figure this out."

EXERCISE: ARE YOU AN ENCOURAGER OR A DISCOURAGER?

Encouraging inspires strength and confidence in another person that she will do her best, helping her believe that she can handle whatever comes. Discouraging diminishes strength and confidence in another person, causing him to believe that his efforts won't be good enough and he cannot handle the outcome.

Encouragers are people who make us feel at ease and good about ourselves. Love and approval are not in question. Reflect on someone in your childhood who helped you feel good about yourself, just as you are. What was his or her magic - what did he or she do that was so encouraging?

Write down a list of those characteristics.

Now, think of the discouragers. They're the people who made you feel uncomfortable, self-conscious, nervous, not good enough, not acceptable as you were. Many of us discourage unknowingly, and this activity will bring to light some of the possible ways that happens. Reflect on a person in your childhood who discouraged you. What was it about that person - what did he or she do that was so discouraging?

Create a list of those discouraging characteristics.

Now, when you find yourself in a challenging situation with your child, tap into this memory of how you were treated. Avoid those discouraging methods and embrace the encouraging methods that had such a positive influence in your own life.

No More "Great Job": How Praise Undermines Self-Esteem

You're on the side of the soccer field on a Saturday afternoon and your nine-year-old daughter, Emma, is charging down the field, dribbling the ball as she goes. "Go Emma go!" you're yelling. It's one of those wonderful moments in a parent's life. Emma closes in on the goal and kicks the ball. She scores! You jump for joy as you see the excitement shining on her face.

"Emma, you were the greatest on that field!" you say when she walks off, her face beet red with effort, at the end of the game. "I'm so proud of you!"

THE DIFFERENCE BETWEEN PRAISE AND ENCOURAGEMENT

We love to heap praise on our children, don't we? It makes us feel so good, and aren't we really helping our kids by making them feel good, too? Aren't we doing it to boost their self-esteem?

This might surprise you, but the praise we love to dole out may not encourage our children to become independent, self-reliant, and self-motivated. It may not boost their self-esteem, either. Look at it this way: If we praise a child only when he is successful, what happens when he's not? His self-esteem can be diminished or hurt.

If you like to praise your children, as so many of us do every single day, we'd like to suggest a different approach. Instead of praising your child, encourage her. We're not saying you should give your child the cold shoulder just when she is coming off that field full of happiness after scoring a goal. Far from it. We want to encourage our children to do their best and flourish in life, but there's a big difference between praise and encouragement.

Let's take a look at this difference. See what the parents say below, and think about how you would feel if you were the child who is showered with praise or with encouragement instead. (We'll call her Tori.)

Praise: "Tori, what a beautiful picture. You are the greatest little artist!"
Encouragement: "You really love art, don't you, Tori? There is a lot happening in this picture. Is there a story that goes with it?"

Praise: "You were great at soccer today. And I was so proud of you when you scored that goal."
Encouragement: "You ran like the wind on that field today,

Tori – looked like you were having a good time. And you must have been feeling pretty pumped when you scored that goal?"

Praise: "You sure know how to please your mom. You did a great job tidying your room!"
Encouragement: "You sure have been doing a lot of work in here. I see you've organized your desk and picked up all of your clothes. It's a pleasure to walk into this room."

Praise: "Boy, I wish everyone was as helpful as you are, Tori. You did a good job clearing the dirty dishes for me."
Encouragement: "Thank you, Tori. When we all contribute, kitchen cleanup goes much faster."

We do an exercise in our class in which some parents play the role of Tori and get showered with praise. Others are encouraged instead. How did the parents who were praised feel? Their response was not what you might imagine:

"I felt I had to keep up my performance," one parent said. "It felt good to be put on a pedestal, but what if I'm not as good next time? I felt judged by you. I felt the need to please you. I felt patronized."

Others said they suspected their parent was using flattery to manipulate them. The praise sounded insincere. It was all about the parent being in charge. They felt they had to please their parent.

Then the other parents who played the role of the child showered with encouragement told us how they felt:

"I felt noticed, acknowledged for my efforts."
"I felt my parent was genuinely interested in me and what I was doing."
"I was more engaged in a conversation with my parent."
"I felt respected, as though I could decide for myself whether I did a good job."
"I felt no pressure to please my parent."

HOW PRAISE CAN LEAD TO JUDGMENT

So what's the difference? When we praise, saying things like, "You were great! Good job!" or, "I was so proud of you!" we are judging and elevating our kids. The focus is on the end result, and praise is the reward for good behavior and a successful performance. The parent is trying to boost the child's sense of worthiness by motivating him to perform at a high level. In the end, the parent is judging the child.

Parents who encourage are not judging their child. Instead, they are motivating her by focusing on her innate love of learning and doing her best. This frees the child to explore and be creative and diminishes her fear of failure. The child won't feel that her worthiness is in question. She will learn to evaluate for herself whether she did a good job or not.

Encouragement places the emphasis on the process and the effort, so it can be given at any time, even when a child is struggling.

MAGIC BULLET
Reinforcing Self-Esteem

Here are eight easy ways to keep your child's self-esteem intact:

1. Think of what you can do or say to communicate that your child is loved, no matter what he does.
2. Seek opportunities to separate the deed from the doer by focusing on your child's effort, not putting her on a pedestal for it. Can you come up with an example in your family life?
3. Greet your child with love and a hug three times today.
4. Turn a negative label for your child into an asset. You could think of a "stubborn" child as "determined," for example, or a "quiet" child as "reflective or thoughtful."
5. Keep asking your child for his ideas and opinions.
6. Carve out some one-on-one time today with your child.
7. Decide, together, ways your child can contribute in the home.
8. Spot improvement or effort and acknowledge it. Put the emphasis on "that" instead of on "you" in your comment to your child.

Say your son's relay team placed third in the race. Here's an encouraging thing to say:

> *"You were really disappointed to lose after you practiced so hard, and yet you were a good sport about it when you went over and congratulated the other teams."*

The focus is on doing your best, not just winning or losing.

PRAISE, ENCOURAGEMENT, AND PERFORMANCE

The difference between praise and encouragement is so significant that it can even affect a child's performance in school. This was illustrated by a study discussed in an article by Po Bronson "The Power (and Perils) of Praise – How Not to Talk to Your Child." The study, run by Carol Dweck, looked at the effect of praise on four hundred children in grade five who were asked to do some puzzles and other activities. Half of the students were praised for their intelligence. They were told, "You must be really smart at this." The other half were praised for their effort: "You worked really hard at this."

The results were significant: Ninety percent of the kids who were told they had worked hard chose the harder tasks in a second round. They got very involved and were willing to try every solution. They significantly improved their skills during the testing and had fun.

Of those who were told they were smart, the majority chose the easier tasks. They quit more readily and looked for much more help and feedback from adults. The "smart" kids played it safe and were anxious.

The study clearly demonstrates that words and labels are powerful. They affect the way children perceive themselves, which in turn affects the way they behave. Focusing on effort rather than innate ability also gives children a sense of control – they can see a direct relationship between effort and results.

We know it's hard to break old habits. It's hard to stop saying, "Oh, I think you're the greatest! I'm so proud of you!" As parents, many of us grew up as praise junkies. But we can try to add more encouragement into the mix, and as time goes by, we'll find we are encouraging more than we are praising. That's a step forward! Here are some new habits to develop:

Avoid phrases that elevate the child such as "You were good, you were great, you were super." Use words that describe what you see or a quality you notice, such as "You were persistent, fair, focused, helpful." Even better, place the focus on "that" instead of on "you":

"That is what I call being determined."
"That was a wonderful thing to do for your sister."

Focus on the child's effort and learning, not on the parent's approval. Avoid phrases such as "I love it when you ..." or "You make me proud when you ..."

Be honest and heartfelt and in the moment. Don't encourage in order to manipulate behavior. Try non-verbal communication – an acknowledging smile or a short note.

THE DIFFERENCE BETWEEN CREATIVITY AND PRODUCTIVITY

When we're being creative, we don't know the outcome. We're exploring and discovering. A child playing with Lego is using her imagination to build all sorts of new objects, such as spaceships and castles. A child painting on an empty canvas will create his own unique vision of a tree or flower. He will either be pleased with the outcome or not, but the pleasure of exploring and learning will not be diminished.

When we're being productive, we already know the outcome of the things we're doing. These are the tried and true things in our life, such as making a bed.

Encouragement helps reinforce the fundamental concept of separating the deed from the doer. We want our children to learn that performance goes up and down, approval from others goes up and down, and the feelings associated with success and failure go up and down. However, our worthiness does not go up and down. We are always worthy. So when we are responding to our children's performance, it's important that we pay attention to what we say as well as how we say it.

OUR PARENTING JOURNEY

A CONFESSION FROM BEVERLEY

When our first-born came along, we thought she was pretty darn smart and we praised her for just about everything she did. And for a very good reason ... we thought that it was our

PRAISE VS. ENCOURAGEMENT

Spot the difference between two parents responding to identical situations. Which approach feels more sincere, more engaging, and more comfortable?

Praise:

"You are the best runner ever!"
"You got an A on the math test. You are so smart!"
"I can't believe it. You went on the potty – I am so proud of you!"
"What a great job you did making your bed. Now you can have a treat!"
"I like it when you clean up so nicely."
"You are such a good boy. I love you!"
"Wow, you ate all your dinner – I am so proud of you!"
"Mom and Dad are so happy with you when you listen and we get out of the house on time."

Encouragement:

"You ran like the wind on the field today! It looked like you were having a great time."
"You got an A on your math test – you must have worked really hard!"
"You went on the potty twice today. Are you feeling pretty good about that?"
"You made your bed all by yourself. Give me five! You must be feeling proud of yourself."
"The toys and books are all picked up. What a difference a clean room makes!"

> *"I love you just the way you are!"*
> *"Wow, you ate all your dinner. You must have been very hungry!"*
> *"Everyone's been cooperating this morning, and now we're going to get to school on time!"*

job and that her self-esteem depended on it! Her day was loaded with our evaluations:

"Great tower you built!"

"What a great little eater you are!"

"Look at how many words you can say. You're such a smart girl."

By the time she was three years old, I noticed that if things didn't come quickly to her, she'd give up and say, "I'm not good at this." On top of that, we found her becoming increasingly dependent on our approval. We had the makings of a praise junkie on our hands.

I recognized the pattern – I'd been there, done that. I, too, was hooked on the approval of others as a child. So I was determined that my daughter would not fall into the same trap.

EXERCISE: ENCOURAGEMENT

Take the challenge and practice these exercises at home. (They're great for the workplace, too!)

Start by choosing two specific encouragements for your child. Write them down.

Now say these encouraging words to your child every day for ten days.

What were the results? Did you notice any change, such as a different reaction or behavior from your child?

How did this practice affect you?

Key things to remember:

- Encouragement is non-judgmental (that means avoiding words like good, great, super, and, instead, using words that describe what you see: persistent, fair, focused, helpful, excited).
- Encouragement is honest and heartfelt and in the moment (not offered to manipulate or change behavior).

- Encouragement is powerful when it is private. A quiet voice or note can work better than a public announcement.
- Encouragement can be non-verbal: an acknowledging smile, or a note tucked into their lunch box, in their coat pocket, or under their pillow.

We were first introduced to this simple way to make encouragement a daily practice by Jody McVittie, M.D. Here's how it sounds: practice with your own words.

1. Descriptive Encouragement:
I noticed how hard you've been working, I see you are interested in ______, I noticed you helping ______.

2. Appreciative Encouragement:
I appreciated your help today. I appreciated your idea. Thank you for your patience at the store.

3. Assuring Encouragement:
I believe you can handle this, I have seen you do things that are harder than this, I have confidence that you can figure this out.

The Power of "Hmm, Uh-huh, I See": How to Really Listen to Your Child

"Hey Ronnie, how are you? What were you up to today?" Ronnie slouches up the stairs and mumbles a one-word answer – "nothing."

Eleven-year-old Maria slides into the car at the end of a school day and complains that her best friend, Rani, was telling stories about her and saying hurtful things. She complains that Rani is no longer her best friend and she never wants to see her again.

Her mother starts asking her questions about what happened and what she did; Maria crosses her arms and falls silent.

THE ART OF LISTENING

We're eager to hear about our child's day, but she doesn't want to talk to us. What's going on? We get this question all the time, from parents of children of all ages.

Listening is a subtle art. It took us as parents a long time to realize this ourselves, and two of the books that have influenced many of the ideas we share in this chapter to improve your listening skills are *Parent Effectiveness Training* by Dr. Thomas Gordon and *How to Talk So Kids Will Listen and Listen So Kids Will Talk* by Adele Faber and Elaine Mazlish. The following exercise is influenced by the latter book. This time, to illustrate the art of listening, we're not going to ask you to role play the child. Instead, imagine that you go to a friend and complain about your mother-in-law. You want her to commiserate.

"She's driving me crazy."
"She's always coming over uninvited, and she gives us nonstop advice on what we're doing wrong with the kids. I've had it!"

Let's play out different answers your friend might give you. After reading each one, write down your gut reaction:

"Come on, it can't be that bad. You're lucky she takes an interest. My in-laws are too busy with their own lives to even notice their grandkids!"

"I guess that's the luck of the draw. You have to learn to take it in your stride."

"You know what I think you should do? Tell her that you have the right to your own privacy and you would appreciate her calling ahead before coming over in the future!"

"What did you do to turn her off so much? Have you made an effort to improve the relationship?"

"You know, I can understand her behavior. She's probably bored and is looking for a way to contribute."

"Poor you. I'd shoot myself if I had to put up with that!"

"Boy, that sounds tough. It's even harder when it involves family!"

Which response would encourage you to open up? Chances are, it was the last one. If we could put a label on that answer, it would be *empathetic*.

Empathy means "understanding and appreciating another person's feelings." This requires us to listen to our child, really listen, without forming an opinion while he's trying to make his point, interrupting before he has a chance to finish, or judging him. To do this, we need to be quiet inside and just listen to what he says.

HOW OVERPROTECTION BLOCKS LISTENING

It sounds easy. Yet many parents, if they were to listen to themselves as they speak to their children, would find they do not just sit and listen. What do they do? They're quick to respond to their children with an answer that actually blocks further discussion. It's not their intent, of course; parents want their kids to talk about their day. Yet they inadvertently end the conversation. Let's see how this works.

> *An eight-year-old child storms into the kitchen after school and starts complaining about her teacher. "I have the worst teacher in the world," she says. "She's so mean. She moved me to another seat in the classroom for no reason!"*
>
> *"It's no use complaining," a parent might say. "All teachers do that."*

What's wrong here? The parent is denying her feelings. Over time the child may think:

> *"What's the point of talking to you? You don't care about my feelings."*

Here's another bestseller:

"Come on now, you must have done something for her to move you. Were you talking to your friends again during class?"

Now the parent is asking questions that deliver a clear message: "You were wrong." It suggests that the parent has no confidence in the child. The parent has dropped the B from the principle of LRB.

Or, how about this:

"Do you know how hard it is to handle a class of twenty-eight kids? She's a saint in my books."

This time the parent is defending the other person, the teacher. The child may think, *This hurts. My own parent doesn't understand. She's not on my side!*

Parents who are overprotective or love solving other peoples' problems will relate to this one:

"You know what I think you should do? Go in to class early tomorrow and tell your teacher that you are sorry and that you will stop being disruptive in class."

This time, the message is that the parent has all the answers and that the child isn't capable of coming up with a solution on her own.

Here's one more:

"Poor you. You must have been mortified. Do you want me to call and talk to her about how she treated you?"

Showing pity can leave anyone feeling inadequate and hopeless.

REFLECTIVE LISTENING

So what's a better way? To illustrate, we recruited a wonderful parent, bestselling author, and media personality, Gill Deacon, to help. We asked Gill to play the eight-year-old who's complaining bitterly about her teacher. Beverley took on the role of parent in this scene:

Gill: "I have the worst teacher in the world. She's so mean. She moved me to another seat in the classroom for no reason!"
Beverley: "Boy, you sound pretty frustrated with your teacher today."
Gill: "I am. She always picks on me and won't listen when ..."

After Gill finished, we asked her how she felt. Here's what the eight-year-old version of Gill said:

"You really care; my feelings matter to you. I feel safe to open up, and I feel heard. And the interesting thing is that the more

I open up, the better I feel. I'm starting to think I'll figure this out – it's not such a big deal anymore."

This is the power of reflective listening. All you do is mirror back to the child how he or she may be feeling. "You sound frustrated." This lets the child know you care and you are listening. You understand how your child feels. Then the ball is back in the child's court, where it belongs. You can continue to practice this reflective listening as your child opens up. "It was that bad? ... Sounds like you had a tough day."

Sounds easy, right? So why do so many of us jump in with answers that block conversation instead of just listening, as the empathetic listener would do? Chalk it up, once again, to human nature. Parents have a primal need to see their children survive and be socially successful in life. If the future is in doubt, we have a fast and furious reflex to protect our child. When we hear about trouble or mistakes at school where we have no control, it's natural to allow the fear reflex to kick in and take over. That's when we might jump in with advice or other comments.

They can easily come out the wrong way. When our child comes home with a C in math, for instance, we might snap:

"When are you going to learn? Why can't you just study like you're supposed to!"

Or, when his teacher tells us that our ten-year-old son got into trouble for causing a ruckus at school, we might say:

"If you can't behave in school at this age, what are you going to be like as a teenager?"

Our angry outburst masks our fear. These reactions are rarely helpful in any situation, but when we talk to our children in this way, it can do outright damage. This sort of tone can put them on the defensive and create distance. If, on the other hand, we explain to our children that we care for them and we're concerned for their future, it's easier for them to understand our fears and easier for us to move past them.

MAGIC BULLET
Listen!

When I ask you to listen to me
And you start giving me advice,
You have not done what I asked.
When I ask you to listen to me
And you begin to tell me "why" I shouldn't feel that way,
You are trampling on my feelings.

When I ask you to listen to me
And you feel you have to do something to
solve my problems,
You have failed me, strange as that may seem.

Listen! All I ask is that you listen;
Not talk, nor do – just hear me.
And I can do for myself – I am not helpless.

Maybe discouraged and faltering, but not helpless.
When you do something for me that I can
and need to do for myself,
You contribute to my fear and weakness.

But when you accept as a simple fact that I do feel
what I feel,
No matter how irrational,
Then I quit trying to convince you
And can get about the business of understanding
What's behind this irrational feeling.
When that's clear,
The answers are obvious and I don't need advice.
Irrational feelings make sense when we
Understand what's behind them.

Perhaps that's why prayer works, sometimes for
some people;
because God is mute, and doesn't give
advice to try to "fix" things.
"He/she" just listens, and lets you work it out
for yourself.

So please listen, and just hear me, and if you
want to talk,
Wait a minute for your turn,
And I'll listen to you.

–Anonymous

HOW TO LISTEN TO YOUR CHILD

Here are four listening tips from Adele Faber and Elaine Mazlish that you may find helpful:

1. You can listen quietly and attentively.
2. You can acknowledge their feelings with a word.
3. You can give the feeling a name.
4. You can give the child his wishes in fantasy.

1. LISTEN QUIETLY WITH FULL ATTENTION

Full attention means you are emotionally, physically, and mentally available to your child, all at the same time. It sounds easy, but we find we have to make a conscious effort to do it. It's not just a question of putting aside the cell phone or computer. We really try to avoid forming an opinion while our child is talking. The goal is to not interrupt him with our thoughts, even if we know what he's trying to say. We just listen, quietly. Only then does a child, or anyone, feel truly heard. It also sends the message that we have confidence in them to own this problem.

We know it's not easy for young parents, especially at dinner time. When you're making dinner, you need to answer the phone, and you have an infant on your hip, your five-year-old isn't going to feel like a priority. The key is to make the time when you can. When you feel that a child needs a few uninterrupted moments, book a time for him or her. You might say:

"I really want to hear what you have to say. Let me finish changing your brother and then I'm all yours."
"When we get home, I want to put away my coat and then sit down and hear all about your day."

2. ACKNOWLEDGE THEM WITH A WORD

When your child is sharing a problem with you, acknowledging them can sound like this: "Oh ... Mmm ... I see ..." (This is called the psychiatrist grunt.) It simply lets the child know that you hear him, you're paying attention, and you're interested in what he has to say.

This also is very helpful with teens. We've spent many an hour sitting on a kitchen stool with a daughter walking in circles around us as she shares the most recent drama in her life. All she needs from us is "Uh-huh ... I see ... That bad?"

Hold Off on the Advice

We naturally want to spare our child pain and trouble by offering advice on how to avoid the problem in the first place. But hold off. When you restrain yourself, you send a positive message: "When I don't take charge of her problems, I'm showing faith that she can figure this out." It's a vote of confidence in her. If she wants our suggestions, and many times she will, she can always ask.

What do you do with a child who wants you to solve things for him? If you want the child to develop belief in his ability to cope and deal with his own issues, you might say:

"Sounds like you're pretty upset. What do you think you can do about it?"
"That's a bummer. What's your plan?"

This is not easy because it's so tempting to dole out advice. To counter this, we need to remind ourselves: Who needs the practice for solving life's challenges – our child or us? We can always be a safety net and a resource for them while they're developing their life skills and confidence.

3. GIVE THEIR FEELINGS A NAME

Even though this sounds straightforward, parents often struggle with it a bit. So let's walk through a scene: You're going out for the evening and you have a child in distress because you're leaving. Many parents say, "You'll be fine. I'll be back soon, don't worry." This kind of response rarely gets the desired results. The child usually gets more upset and clingy. Why? You've just denied his feelings. Now he has to ramp up the volume to convince you that you're wrong, he can't handle it!

Instead, you might say this:

"Sounds like you're sad that Daddy is going out. Is that how you're feeling?"

You're calling it like you see it by giving the feeling a name. Your child now thinks, *Dad really understands what I am trying to say*. There isn't the need to convince anymore. This helps younger children develop their feeling language, too.

You can then ask your child what would help him handle your departure better. Get him to focus on solutions instead of complaining. A promise to give him another kiss goodnight when you get home is sometimes all it takes.

4. HEAR THE WISH AND SHARE IT

This is a favorite tip. Let's return to the scene where you are going out for the evening and your child is howling. You can say this:

> *"I wish there were two Daddies, one to stay here with you and one to go out with Mommy."*

This tool is particularly powerful with young children. It validates their feelings and builds on their imagination. And it works like crazy.

When Beverley's son was three, he went into a full-throttle meltdown because his sister had just poured the last of the Cheerios into her bowl. Beverley pulled out her imaginary wand:

> *"Andrew, I wish I had a magic wand, and I'd fill this room with Cheerios for you. You'd be covered in Cheerios."*

He stopped his fit, grinned, and ran to give her a hug.

This is the magic of listening. When we do it right, we're offering our child the chance to share, vent, explain himself, and be heard. When this happens, a child will feel less upset, less confused, and more able to cope. She'll know you have the

MAGIC BULLET
Top Ten Listening Tips

How to really listen when your child comes to you with an issue, a problem or a grievance:

1. Set aside distractions.
2. Listen and wait. Nod and say, "Hmmm, uh-huh, I see."
3. Match your facial expression to theirs – shocked eyes, wide open mouth, smile, raised eyebrows, pout.
4. Ask for clarification. "Really? She said that? Wow!"
5. Realize that you are most likely getting an unrefined version of the story and most certainly a biased one. Stay calm.
6. Empathize. "Ooh, sounds like you felt it was unfair, upsetting, hurtful ..." Empathizing does not mean you agree with the child. (This is particularly helpful to remember when you are the subject of the complaint.) Validate and name emotions – embarrassment, fear, disappointment, anxiety.
7. Give a sense of perspective. "On a scale of 1 to 10, how big a problem is it?"
8. Ask what their plan is. "What do you want to do about it?"
9. Offer to brainstorm. "Do you need my help? Can I suggest something?"
10. Offer comfort. "How about a hug?"

confidence in her ability to solve the problem on her own. It's true for adults, too. Just remember how you feel after you've had the chance to share a problem with a close friend. If she really listened, you had a chance to talk and be heard. You probably felt better for it.

As Faber and Mazlish say, "When we acknowledge a child's feelings, we do him a great service. We put him in touch with his inner reality. And once he's clear about that reality, he gathers the strength to begin to cope."

To summarize, here are the key benefits of good, effective listening:

- Children learn that you're a safe place to turn to.
- Talking helps them sort through their feelings, which can be calming.
- Through the process of sharing, they clarify their thoughts and hopefully get ready to deal with the problem themselves.

EXERCISE: AWARENESS, AWARENESS, AWARENESS

It's important to listen to ourselves, too. According to the National Science Foundation, we have about 50,000 thoughts per day. Because many of these thoughts dwell on the past and the future and easily descend into the negative, it's important to be aware of them - a process that is referred to as mindfulness.

If you have negative self-talk as a parent, either about yourself or your child, review the following elements of mindfulness:

1. Awareness of the stimulus or situation and the accompanying feelings. Write down a current negative thought or feeling.

2. Awareness of the beliefs and values that you hold from childhood. Possibly "How well you perform determines your worth," or, "You'll never be good enough." Write it down.

3. Awareness that you can change your belief system now that you are aware of its negative, hurtful impact. Thoughts such as, "I am valued and worthwhile," or "My parents would not have wanted me to feel inadequate." Write it down.

Bribes and Threats Are Out and Cooperation Is In

Now that we have mastered the listening skills that will help our children with their feelings, it's time to focus on our feelings and what upsets us, such as messy rooms, bedtime battles and homework showdowns. It's fine to have the goal of making your home a happier, more collaborative place. But how can that be done when there are so many differences and conflicting priorities under one roof? This chapter will give you some practical tips on how to make it happen.

GIVE KIDS MORE LEEWAY

One of the best ways to improve your home environment is to give kids more leeway in making decisions about their lives. Children, like all of us, want to be respected. They want to have a say in what happens. If they don't get it, they'll find lots of creative ways to fight us for it. Remember, this is a good thing. They're trying to tell us something: "I'm ready to have more independence and make more decisions in my life."

Why not let them? We encourage our children to make as many decisions about their lives as possible – age appropriate decisions, that is. A four-year-old, for example, can decide what to wear to school. A six-year-old can make his own sandwich. A twelve-year-old can figure out when she's tired and needs to go to sleep.

We say yes as much as possible. This doesn't mean we say yes every time our child wants a cookie or money to buy another pair of jeans. We don't always say yes to a request for things. We do say yes as often as possible to life experiences.

When kids are able to make decisions about their lives, they get the chance to explore, be creative, and develop confidence in their abilities. They also get closer to achieving the long-term goals of independence, accountability, and resilience, whether that was their plan or not. It's a winning situation for all.

SET LIMITS

There will be limits, though. Freedom doesn't exist in a vacuum. We, as parents, have to set limits. We have to use our judgment to determine those limits, based on our values and each child's readiness. When would that be? It's a hard call to make. Children typically feel they're ready long before we think they are.

Twelve-year-old Harry, for instance, is not the active type; he's a math whiz, and he'd rather be playing games on the computer. His dad thinks sports are important, so he encourages Harry to go to soccer practice, even though his son doesn't feel like it. Now it's midway through the season, and Harry wants to quit.

Harry's father can't make him perform on that field when he doesn't want to, but it may be tempting to tell Harry, "Finish the season, like it or not." It's important to remember the goal. It's to be physically fit and enjoy sports, not to excel in soccer.

Still, Harry's dad doesn't want him to quit and let down his teammates, so he might say, "You are really unhappy with soccer, you hate playing defense, and you don't want to go anymore. But the team is depending on you, and you've made a commitment to the team."

What happens if that doesn't convince? The best bet is to encourage a chat between the coach and Harry. Maybe he can play another position on the field, or learn another skill. If that still doesn't work, perhaps it's time for Harry to pull out. Now Harry and his dad have a chance to problem solve together:

> *"Let's figure out a way to get some fitness in your life that will suit you better."*
>
> *"Let's look at a different sport for next term."*

Harry can be in charge of researching some other activities. Maybe he'll enjoy rugby! What's his best friend involved in? The deal is that once he chooses, he agrees to finish at least one term.

PICK YOUR BATTLES

It's important to pick your battles. We know a ten-year-old girl called Aisha who insists on dropping her clothes on the floor and not picking them up. At first her mother is furious; she badgers Aisha to clean up her clothes, and when that doesn't work, her mother picks them up herself and feels resentful. In a couple of days, the floor is covered again.

We asked the mother two things: Is this a life or death situation? Do you want to hurt your relationship with your daughter over the state of a room?

Her mother decides to let Aisha make this decision. If she wants to leave her clothes on the floor, she can do it. Mom isn't going to complain. But she's going to show self-respect, so she isn't going to pick up the clothes from the floor, either. If Aisha wants her clothes to be cleaned, she can pick them up and put them in the hamper or do her own laundry. As part of the deal, Aisha even agrees to vacuum the floor once a week!

It works just fine, especially when Mom closes the bedroom door so she doesn't have to see the mess.

Hair can be a flashpoint. One mother we know, Kathy, came to class one day in a very sour mood. She had just been to the hair salon with her five-year-old daughter, Emma, and the trip was not a success. Emma had refused a hair cut for six months, and Kathy finally cajoled her into the salon for a haircut the day before a ballet performance. When they got there, Emma balked. "I wanna leave." Soon, all the ladies were staring, and Kathy was getting desperate. She couldn't physically force her little girl to sit in the chair and submit to the scissors. So she resorted to a well-worn trick, saying, "I'll take you to the toy store if you get your hair cut."

The bribe worked, but Kathy was still fuming on the way home from the toy store. Then she switched gears. "You behaved so badly, what do you think your punishment should be?" "I should be grounded for three days," Emma said sweetly. "I really love being grounded. That's the best."

The entire showdown could have been avoided if Kathy had simply given Emma the choice of whether to have her hair cut or not. If she wants to keep her hair long, it may be harder to brush and clean. Kathy and Emma may agree on braids that will keep it in check for a couple of days. But even at five, Emma can take responsibility for brushing her hair herself.

We need to pick our battles. The more decisions we can give to our kids, the better. The more power they have over the small stuff, such as their dirty clothes and messy hair, the more they will cooperate when we make the decisions on the big stuff, such as safety, screen time, and nutrition. They'll cooperate because they'll see that we were respectful and we listened to them.

MORE CHOICE = FEWER POWER PLAYS

Parents sometimes worry that if they give their kids a little power, the kids will want a lot more. In our experience, that's not true. We find that when kids have more control over the choices in their lives, they get their respect and power fix, so they're not as eager to challenge us when it's time for dinner, bed, or the bath. They're more likely to listen to us when we say, "This is important to me."

Now, it's fine to say, "Let them choose." But how? You might consider whether you want to give your kids a broad choice or a narrow one. This depends on what you, the parent, are willing to do.

FIRST THING IN THE MORNING

Here's a simple example for first thing in the morning. You can give kids a broad choice: "What do you want to have for breakfast?" But that may be impractical, especially if you have a number of kids. So you can narrow the choice a bit: "Would you prefer bagels or cereal this morning?" Or narrow it some more: "It's bagel morning. Do you want yours toasted or plain?"

BEDTIME

Let's look at another example, bedtime. This is a broad choice: "When do you want to go to bed?" If you have a younger child, you might offer a more restricted choice: "Do you want to brush your teeth now or after you put on your PJs?" or, "Do you want one long story or two short ones?"

Your eleven-year-old child wants to stay up a half hour later. You think he'll be too tired, but you decide it's good for him to learn to figure out what his body needs for himself. So you let him make that decision and you both agree he'll try it out for one week. By day two, he wakes up pretty grumpy and tired. What do we say in the morning?

Nothing.

We may be thinking:

"If you had only listened to me, you wouldn't be so tired and grumpy this morning."

But we'll resist that urge. Instead, we might wait for him to say something first. Then we can reply:

Hmmm ... you're feeling that sleepy, are you? Yeah, it mustn't feel very good.

We have to have confidence that our children can figure out when their bodies need more sleep. We had a dad who did this with his six-year-old. On day three, his son walked into the house and headed straight for his bed and collapsed, coat and shoes still on. He slept right through to the next morning and never argued with Dad about bedtime again.

HOMEWORK

Our role is to support our children and set the stage for a productive night of homework. The goal is not to nag and badger them to do their homework, but instead to work collaboratively on how homework will be handled. We might work on establishing a routine together, or we might offer them some choices:

"Do you want to do your homework now or right after dinner?"
"Alone, or with some help?"
"With music, or without?"

BATH TIME

One of our parents said his two kids, ages three and five, loved playing in the bathtub so much that they gave him a struggle every time he tried to get them out. Then one night he gave them freedom of choice, telling them, "You can stay in the bathtub as long as you like." They stayed there until the bathwater got cold, and by the time they finally came out, their teeth were chattering. It never happened again.

HOW TO HELP KIDS BE RESILIENT

One of our jobs as parents is to protect our children. Sometimes, however, helping them build immunity by exposing them to certain risks is the best protection.

Here are three tips to help children who don't do well with new situations become more resilient:

- Be incompetent so that they become competent. Children soon learn that once they survive the initial struggle, they'll manage better with time and practice.
- Explore various options together, along with the pros and cons – and only contribute your ideas as a last resort.

- Resist the temptation to protect your child from the results of her choices. Even if your child is unhappy at times, she is learning that uncomfortable feelings can be endured, dealt with, and eventually overcome.

EXERCISE: ROADBLOCKS TO EFFECTIVE COMMUNICATION

1. Read aloud the following things parents typically say to children when they are frustrated and fill out the questions.

Blame: *"What have you been doing up here? I told you, we don't have time to fool around this morning. The trouble with you is you never listen!"*

Pretend you are a child receiving this message. How do you feel?

Micromanage: *"I need you to go upstairs, brush your teeth, wash your face, and get into your pajamas. Then it is story time."*

Again, as a child receiving this message, how do you feel?

Demand: *"I don't care if you are watching TV. Turn it off now! Get your backpack ready. What are you waiting for?"*

As a child receiving this message, how do you feel?

Compare: *"Why can't you be more like your sister? She's two years younger than you, and she's always ready on time."*

As a child receiving this message, how do you feel?

Threaten: *"If you don't come down right now, there will be no dinner for you."*

As a child receiving this message, how do you feel?

Scoff: *"You knew you had a test tomorrow and you left your book at school. Brilliant!"*

As a child receiving this message, how do you feel?

Control: *"No, you can't go for a sleepover tonight. You need your rest."*

As a child receiving this message, how do you feel?

Criticize: *"What is the matter with you? Can't you remember even the simplest thing?"*

As a child receiving this message, how do you feel?

Punish: *"You stay in your room until I tell you to come out."*

As a child receiving this message, how do you feel?

Give in: *"Do what you want, I'm tired of fighting with you."*

As a child receiving this message, how do you feel? Did you feel happy or hurt?

2. Summarize your answers to the questions above: How did this impact your self-esteem?

What did you think about your parent?

Was LRB on the radar screen?

3. Circle the roadblocks above that currently impede good communication with your child. Now take our challenge and do and say something new next time you find yourself having a difficult moment. Better yet, make a promise not to say anything discouraging for one hour and build on that!

Give Peace a Chance: Ten Techniques for Defusing Family Power Struggles

"I find it hard to stop yelling," one of our parents shared in class one morning. "I'm aware of it, and yet I keep doing it. When I lower my voice, it sounds unnatural. And then the kids say, 'Where's Mom gone?'"

We both felt that way during the years we were trying to get our children to do things. Yelling is no fun. It's not what we planned when we became parents, but somehow we found ourselves raising our voices more than we liked. We hadn't yet become aware of our subconscious feelings or realized the pressure we felt to be and be seen as successful parents.

PREVENTING POWER STRUGGLES

We found that when we tried to prevent struggles before they began, we yelled less and our kids started cooperating more. It was truly a win-win.

When we feel ourselves "about to lose it," we might remember that we're about to role model a disrespectful, out-of-control adult to our children. We are showing them what adults do when they don't get their way. We're sending the completely wrong message!

A good way to rectify this is to look at the hot spots in our day: mornings, mealtimes, homework, and bedtime. These are the times of the day we are most pressured and can easily get angry and go into dictator mode. We think, *I can't be late for work*, or, *I won't be able to hold it together if I don't get my child into bed on time tonight!*

What else is going through our heads at moments like this?

"You aren't going to get away with it this time!"
"Oh yes you will, young man!"
"Why can't you just listen for a change?"
"That's it. I've had it!"

And what's our child thinking?

"You can't make me."
"Why do you always get to decide?"
"It's not fair."
"I can do what I want."

Notice again the disconnect between parent and child. The parent says, "He doesn't listen to me," but, in fact, the child can hear perfectly well. He's listening, but, like most of us, he doesn't

DOONE'S POWER STRUGGLE: A Confession

When my daughter, Morgan, was ten, she called from school one day and asked if she could go to her friend Emma's house. I said no, because she had too much to do.

Morgan came home unhappy. She turned to me and said, "Next time you tell me I can't go to Emma's house, you're going to have a consequence. I'm not going to tell you I'm going to her house!"

want to be told what to do. Submission would place him in an inferior position and make him feel hurt and powerless.

Parent and child have one thing in common, though – how they both feel at a time like this. Both can feel hurt, angry, provoked, challenged, or powerless when they're defeated.

THE PREVENTATIVE, SHARING MINDSET

We want to prevent situations like this before they occur. Prevention starts with a mindset. We want to drop the old controlling parenting model, in which we put ourselves in a position of superiority and use power over our children, whether by managing and directing them or calling the shots. This model sets us up for a power struggle with our kids.

The problem is the power imbalance. That's why even the permissive pushover model, in which we abdicate control and give power to the child, can lead to a power struggle. Parent or child gets fed up with the power imbalance, and the struggle begins. This can also happen when we happily pamper a child and he becomes entitled.

Sharing power with our children helps create relationships based on cooperation and equality. Lots of parents find the idea of sharing power hard to grasp, though. After all, aren't we older and more experienced? How can an eight-year-old know what's best?

We think that not only is it possible to share power and responsibility but it is also downright beneficial to treat children with respect. It helps them take steps toward long-term goals, such as the ability to solve problems and be independent. It helps them develop "copability." It even helps us get through the day.

TECHNIQUES FOR DEFUSING POWER STRUGGLES

Here's a handy list of our favorite techniques to defuse power struggles before they begin.

1. LET ROUTINES BE THE BOSS, NOT YOU

Ask, "What do we do in our house before breakfast?" Be quiet and let the child take the next step. If your child resists the established routine, it is time for a meeting to plan a morning routine satisfactory to all. Routines work best when the child has a say, we are consistent, and we follow through. If everybody agrees to be dressed before breakfast and someone goofs around, he might leave for school on an empty stomach. Natural consequences can be wonderful life lessons if parents don't interfere by giving endless warnings or by bailing out their children.

2. FOCUS ON THE NEEDS OF THE SITUATION

When you say, "It's leaving time in five minutes," you're just stating a fact. You're not giving an order or your personal opinion. The needs of the family are running the show here, which is a great way to avoid power struggles. By stating the needs of the situation or pointing out the routine in a matter-of-fact, impersonal way, you can avoid a lot of problems – and get through the day more cooperatively. Here are some more examples:

> *"Crayons aren't for throwing; balls are for throwing.*
> *"That's Daddy's book. Here's a book for you."*

This gives your child an alternative and redirects him to appropriate behavior.

> *"Time is up for TV today."*

You're stating it impersonally.

> *"Chairs are for sitting on, not for standing on."*

Give your child straight information; then, if necessary, move the child calmly and without words.

"It's tidy up time, then it's story time."

You're describing a routine. When limits are stated this way, the child has less to rebel against, so he's more likely to cooperate.

3. GIVE LIMITED CHOICES

Ask, "Do you want to get your clothes on upstairs, or bring them down here?" If your child is using power or testing you, it helps to give him a limited choice because he makes the decision – not you! The trick is to give limited choices that you can live with.

4. SHOW YOU UNDERSTAND AND YOU CARE

Ask, "Are you having a rough morning?" Offer a hug. Closeness when a child is expecting distance can be very powerful. It shows you believe in her and you see that she is having a bad moment.

5. LET YOUR FEET DO THE TALKING, NOT YOUR MOUTH

Hold out your hand and lead the child calmly upstairs to get dressed for school. If you have to say anything, talk about the weather, not about what he is to do! Do it in a pleasant, non-accusatory way. How you do it is just as important as what you do.

6. ASK FOR YOUR CHILD'S HELP

When in doubt, ask your child what to do. Children love to be resources for us. It makes them feel that they are valued and their ideas appreciated. You might say, "I need your help to decide what we could serve for dinner when Grandma comes this weekend." Or, you might ask your kids to show you how to use your remote or your new computer.

7. GIVE YOUR CHILD A JOB

Your children have more time and energy than you do, so why do everything for them? Because it is faster and better? Perhaps. But that is short-term thinking. Doing things around the house helps children feel more in control and more capable. It is power over the situation instead of power over others. Much more effective.

8. USE A RESPECTFUL TONE OF VOICE

Tone of voice conveys a lot. A calm and respectful approach, with no hint of blame, is much more effective than an angry or impatient tone. You might consider using the same tone you'd use with a friend in the same situation.

9. PREVIEW

You can talk to kids ahead of time so they're not surprised when they have to rush to the pool after school or come home from the playground in time for dinner with their grandparents. If your child has a swimming lesson after school on Thursday, you might consider previewing the afternoon ahead of time:

MAGIC BULLET
Say What *You're* Going to Do

Tell the kids what you are going to do, not what they should do.

We used to say things like this:

> *"You have only five minutes to get ready to go, so hurry up. Get your shoes on. Where's your coat?"*
> *"Would you two stop bugging each other. It's hard to read the story with all this noise."*
> *"Stop talking to me that way – it's rude!"*
> *"You left a mess in the kitchen. Would you get in there now and clean it up!"*

But this approach backfired, because it steered us straight for a power struggle with our kids. Then, instead of telling the kids what they should do, we said what we were going to do. Here's what this sounds like:

> *"It's leaving time in five minutes. I am going to brush my teeth and then get ready to go."*
> *"I will continue reading the story when everyone is listening."*
> *"You must be upset about something to talk to me that way. Do you want to tell me about it?"*

> *"I'm happy to get dinner started when the kitchen is cleaned up."*
>
> The difference in our children was dramatic. The new way involved less talk and less blame. It allowed them to determine for themselves what needed to be done.

"How much time do you need to get ready? What do you need to put in your backpack for this afternoon?"

This approach is especially helpful if you're trying to avoid meltdowns in the morning. You can sit down with your child in a quiet moment and ask:

"What time do you need to get up? Would you like an alarm clock, or shall I wake you? Is that enough time to do everything you need to do in the morning?"

This technique can also help if your young child usually resists when it's time to leave the playground, a play date at a friend's, or the toy store. What do you do when your child refuses to leave the playground? You can give him a five-minute warning and ask him how he would like to fill that time.

"Do you want to go on the swing or play in the sandbox?"

Ask for his agreement to leave at the end of the five minutes. If he still refuses to leave, it's best to wait it out and not force him. This is a training time. Empathetic words can help.

> *"It's hard to leave the park when you're having such a good time. We can come back tomorrow if you'd like."*

Once you get home, taking away television for the evening may make you feel more in control of the situation, but it will not solve the problem. Pick a quiet time, after dinner or just before lights out, for example, and ask your child what was going on at the playground.

> *"You didn't feel that you had enough time to do everything you wanted to do today? Did you think Dad was rushing you? What do you think we could do next time to fix this?"*

Before the next trip to the playground, have another previewing session and get his agreement up front. Remind him of your discussion and why you have to leave when you do. Use the five-minute warning again. Transitions take practice!

10. MIX IT UP

You can pick and choose from these techniques to deal with most potential conflicts in a way that prevents power struggles.

For example, your seven-year-old hasn't picked up her toys off the family room floor, and it's time for bed. Instead of nagging, you might describe what you see:

"I see toys waiting to be put away."

Then be quiet and disengage, giving your child room to deal with it. There's no point in hovering, glaring, or tapping your foot. That will only invite resistance from your child and set off a power struggle.

Instead, you can use another one of these techniques. You might, for instance, ask a question to help the child focus on the needs of the situation or the routine. Get down to the child's level, establish eye contact, and say:

"What is it we do before stories in our house?"
"It's five minutes to story time. Is there anything you need to do to be ready?"
"This looks like a big job. Would you like five minutes of my help? What do you want me to pick up? What will you pick up?"

If they stop tidying and start lounging around or playing, say:

"I see you're not ready. Call me when you are."

You might even tell them what you'll be doing:

"Mommy's going upstairs to get ready for stories."

How we communicate is as important as what we say. Your attitude is clear to your child. The attitude of love, respect, and belief is what children thrive on.

FAMILY MEETINGS

Kids need a voice and a say, and family meetings are a great way to give them this. You can start small and talk about menus for the coming week, what you're going to do at the park on Saturday, what movie you might watch together on Saturday night, and whatever issues seem to be important at the time. This is a good time to talk about challenges, such as screen time on weeknights.

One of our parents said they brought up a bothersome challenge at a family meeting – their young daughter used to wake up the baby by making too much noise going up the stairs to bed. They asked the child if she had any ideas. "Daddy could tiptoe," she said. This was brilliant on her part as now she was not the guilty party, and she could be in charge of Dad!

GROUND RULES

A few ground rules:

1. For best results, have these family meetings at a consistent time each week.
2. Start every meeting on a positive note. Most popular is what we call the "family celebration," when each family member gives and receives words of appreciation.
3. Make your meetings fun, and make them brief! Fifteen minutes may be all your young child can handle.

4. Relax in the family room for your meeting, or, if your children are young, have them crawl into your bed on Saturday morning for the family "powwow."

Someone will be the meeting's chairperson and make sure that everyone's voice gets heard. If you are an intense parent, don't even think about taking on this job! You'll also need a secretary to record family decisions and jobs. Many parents keep a journal just for this reason, and it becomes a family record. They say their kids love looking back at those first attempts at writing words. These jobs are best rotated between family members each week.

End with another celebration of some kind, like a special meal, a family game, or an outing.

Make an agenda. Here are some ideas:

1. Appreciations or thank-yous
2. What went well and what could be improved
3. Family needs for the coming week
4. Family jobs/contributions
5. This week's fun activity
6. Family game/activity time

FAMILY APPRECIATION

The highlight of family meetings happens at the start – the giving and receiving of appreciation. This is a chance for siblings to be positive with one another. It also establishes a wonderful atmosphere in which everyone in the family feels valued and worthwhile.

As parents, we know that appreciating each other is important, but we often forget this in the day-to-day activity of family life. Building this practice into a regular time in the week can be therapeutic for everyone.

The parents can start off with showing appreciation for each other.

"Thank you for taking over at bath time last night. I was really tired and needed the break."
"I love the foot rubs you give me when we watch TV."
"I appreciate all your work trying out new recipes for our dinners lately."

Then, parents can highlight the helpful things the children have done, or share something they enjoy about each child.

"Thanks for giving your brother a hand with his homework this week. That was a real help."
"The baby was fussing and you put on a show for her and made her laugh. She's lucky to have you for a brother."
"I love your big hug every morning."

Then the kids get a shot at it. Their appreciations will likely focus on material things at first, but this will change with experience.

"Thanks for taking us for ice cream today, Dad."
"I appreciate you helping me practice my lines for the play."
"Thanks for switching dishes night with me when I wanted to go to my friends for a sleepover."

Next, turn to family plans or other items on the agenda. These might include dinner menus for the week, a list of jobs kids can do, and a family outing for the coming weekend.

You might notice that conflicts are not on the list. Why? They can turn the meeting negative. It is better to introduce problems very gradually, after the kids have fully bought into these meetings.

By the way, agreement on issues is best reached by consensus, not voting. This can be more challenging, but it keeps kids from ganging up on each other and promotes flexibility.

Parents report that these meetings are great for teaching life skills such as negotiation, respect for others, and open-mindedness. This makes cooperation and community involvement much more feasible!

PLANNING A FAMILY OUTING

This part of the meeting can be fun, so let your imagination flow. Most often there is an obvious winning idea on the list, and the decision is easy. Sometimes the process of elimination works best. If you can't agree, don't let this drag down the whole meeting. Sleeping on it, or asking for the family to find a compromise, often works.

"How about this: If it rains tomorrow, we'll do the movie. And if it's sunny, we'll go to the zoo?"

JOBS AND CONTRIBUTIONS

Together, make a list of jobs to be done around the house – children are more cooperative if they can contribute their ideas. Take a clue from what they like, whether it is cooking, feeding or walking the pet, laundry, cleaning, or outside jobs. Have them pick one thing. Not everybody has to do everything.

Here's a tip: Agree on a time when each task is to be complete. For example, dinner dishes will be done by eight thirty and lunches will be packed the night before.

MAKE TIME FOR TRAINING

When we give a task to a child, training is important. Whether it's setting the table, clearing a dishwasher, or walking to school without an adult, training is not only vital but can be a satisfying experience for both parent and child. If we neglect this step, there's a good chance that we'll spend a lot of energy correcting, redoing, or criticizing their efforts. Then the child may think, *There's no pleasing you*, or, *What's the point? I quit, you do it!*

Take these four steps when you train your child:

1. Show them: Your child signs up for dishwasher duty. Walk them through the steps: scraping, rinsing, what

goes on the upper shelf, and so forth. Even if the child has watched you do this for years, invest this time so you reduce the risk of corrections.

2. Do it together: Next time you and the child do the job together and some instructions are still okay.
3. They show you: The child is now ready to do the job with you observing. Last chance for input!
4. Be a resource: The child owns the job and turns to you if they run into a snag.

Training is important when you give your child new freedoms, too. Your child wants to walk to school without you, and if you're like most parents, you feel nervous. The four steps can actually give you, the parent, confidence that your child is well-prepared for their new responsibility. It sounds like this. As you walk your child to school, help her think through the things she needs to watch out for:

> *"It's important to keep an eye on cars backing out of driveways."*
> *"If you get nervous or run into some trouble, let's identify which neighbors you are comfortable approaching."*
> *"When you get to the crosswalk, make eye contact with the crossing guard and make sure you do a look for yourself, too."*

By step four, you will have much more confidence in your child's readiness and a lot less fear for their safety. So will your child.

AGE APPROPRIATE CONTRIBUTIONS AT HOME

Some families aren't sure which jobs are age appropriate when their children say, "Let me do that!" or, "Can I help?" Here's a list that comes from parents in our classes.

Tasks for two- and three-year-olds:

- Pick up toys and put away
- Dust
- Sweep the floor
- Set the table
- Vacuum
- Help prepare meals
- Scrub vegetables
- Put salad ingredients in bowl
- Stir ingredients
- Help put groceries away
- Empty waste baskets
- Help in garden
- Water the lawn
- Feed pets
- Help clear the table
- Wipe up spills

Tasks for four- and five-year-olds:

- Set the table
- Get cereal and milk (put in a small jug)
- Help plan menus
- Find items at grocery store

- Feed pets
- Help with yard and garden work
- Help make beds
- Help cook (make desserts)
- Help wash the dishes
- Load or empty the dishwasher
- Make sandwiches

Tasks for six- to eight-year-olds:

- Cook simple foods like tortillas and eggs
- Grate cheese
- Peel vegetables
- Prepare own school lunch
- Take pet for a walk
- Do simple ironing
- Straighten and clean out drawers
- Carry in grocery bags

Tasks for nine- and ten-year-olds:

- Mop floors
- Change sheets
- Sew buttons
- Clean backyard furniture
- Read recipes and cook meals
- Bake
- Cut flowers and arrange in vase
- Help with barbecue
- Help with painting
- Polish silver
- Wash car
- Do own laundry

Tasks for eleven- to fifteen-year-olds:

- Mow the lawn
- Look out for younger siblings
- Clean pool
- Barbecue food
- Help build things
- Run errands
- Help in parent's business
- Buy groceries from a list
- Cook meals
- Wash windows
- Change light bulbs
- Make appointments
- Order out for family
- Wash car
- Operate saws for home projects

Tasks for sixteen- to eighteen-year-olds:

- Run errands with car
- Maintain car
- Help with family budgets
- Help younger children with homework
- Handle own checking account
- Take care of house/garden/yard

Remember that work is simply a task that needs to be done and can be learned with pleasure and training. It is useful to reflect on the attitude you model as you do tasks. Is it desire? Or are you showing resentment about doing the dishes or making dinner yet again? Perhaps next time you can radiate the attitude that you feel good when you contribute and that life feels much better when the family's needs are met. You may get some skeptical looks, but that's a sign that the message was received!

SIBLING RIVALRY

"Shut up, you poopoohead!"

This is how Doone's six-year-old, Maddie, greeted her sixteen-year-old brother, Eric, one morning. Eric ignored her and kept eating his cereal.

Then Maddie grabbed Eric's hat and whacked him, just to make sure he noticed. Eric got up and started running after her.

"Mom!" she screamed.

She had awakened a sleeping giant.

It's a common conundrum: "My brother hit me!" "They're so mean to me!" "She took my favorite shirt and she won't give it back!" "She said I'm fat."

The list goes on and on. This is the part of parenting most people don't imagine when they bring home child number two or three. Weren't the kids supposed to be buddies, lifelong friends? Wasn't that the point?

Yet fights between kids are bound to erupt – over screen time, clothes, their fair share of everything.

HOW TO HANDLE SIBLING RIVALRY

So how do we deal with it? The approach we choose will influence how frequent the fights are and how intense they are. Our long-term goal is to eliminate the need to fight and replace it with collaboration between the siblings.

Let's start with a typical scenario.

Jamie, age ten, starts wailing in the family room. His mother rushes in. Jamie's on the floor, writhing. "Harry hit me!"

Harry, age twelve, is sitting in front of the TV, watching his favorite show.

"Harry," the mother says, "Don't hit your brother. Go to your room! Jamie, are you okay? That was a mean thing for your brother to do."

It is only natural to take sides and try to protect the younger child. When we take sides, however, we risk creating and reinforcing the roles of aggressor and victim. The children may come to believe that their parent protects the weaker one and therefore cares for that child more. The aggressor can become labeled as the difficult one, and the message we may inadvertently be sending is that he is the powerful one and not

THE SCALE OF COMPETITION

There are many levels of competition ranging from minor to extreme. The scale starts with comparing. It escalates through bickering, vying, rivalry, conflict, and battle, ending with war.

submissive to his parent. The aggressor may feel good when he's not being submissive, and the victim gets the benefit of the big guns on his side.

Instead of taking sides, it's usually better to put the combatants in the same boat. "You guys are making too much noise for the rest of us (need some time apart, are going to break something, are going to hurt each other)."

Yet many parents find it hard to implement these suggestions, especially when one child appears to have been the punching bag for the other. So let's backtrack for a moment.

TEACHING THEM TO DEAL WITH CONFLICT

Our job is to teach kids to deal with conflict, and dealing with family conflict is a really good way to do this. We don't want to deny our kids the chance to learn this important skill. Instead, we want to help them master it, so they can deal effectively with conflicts when they arise in the playground, at camp, or later in their adult lives.

Sibling rivalry is a competition between kids that creates winners and losers. If we pick the winner and punish the loser, we will only intensify that competition and foster more fighting. What's more, we can be pretty sure that the story we hear from the injured party is only one part of the whole story. We may not know exactly what happened. But what if we do know what happened? We still shouldn't take sides. The key is to look at the big picture and recognize that jealousy and competition and hurt feelings provoke the fighting. So it's better to focus on conflict management and solutions, reducing the need to compete.

If we step in with a solution, we deny kids an important opportunity to learn how to resolve conflict themselves. Here's how this would work in a typical situation. Your eight-year-old daughter, Kim, is standing in front of the TV. She's taunting six-year-old Jon.

"Get out of the way!" he cries. "I can't watch my show! Mom, she's bugging me. She won't let me see my show!"

You're upstairs in the kitchen. You say:

"I'm in the kitchen if you need me."

Children need to know they can go to you for help, but help doesn't come running. Usually, the wounded party shows up first.

"It sounds like you're really frustrated."

You're listening first. You express empathy.

"So what do you want to do about that?"

You're asking your child to solve the problem. You can explore the tools, words, and strategies to use when your child is having a conflict with another child, whether at home or school. For instance, "Tell the other child how you feel," or, "Disengage and go somewhere else or find someone else to be with." "Get help from an adult."

"I've already used my words."
"Okay, what are your other choices? Could you ask in a different way? You can practice on me if you wish."

Chances are, the other child is listening near the door. Be sure to give the other child a vote of confidence, too. We don't want to take sides.

"I know your sister can be fair. Can you try again?"

This is an opportunity to show your child how to appreciate the other's point of view. If a child has lashed out at a sibling, there's a reason. It may have nothing to do with the child who's complaining. The aggressor might be feeling hurt inside because of something that happened at school or in the home. Or it could just be the current state of their relationship.

"Why do you think she's dancing in front of the TV?"

Even young children can be insightful if you ask them a question like this.

"Perhaps she's bored and just wants to play with you?"
"How could you handle this?"

Jon might come up with a solution – he can watch the TV show now and play with Kim right after.

We believe this approach works even when children are hitting and hurting each other. This is a challenging scenario that makes many parents revert to the controlling role. They punish the aggressor and console the injured party. But we think parents should instead focus on understanding the behavior of the child who hit and encourage cooperation and conflict resolution in the household at the same time. Let's see how this plays out.

Jose, age ten, has just punched his eleven-year-old sister, Gabriela. She's wailing and holding her arm.

What do you do? First, you check the injury. It looks like she's going to have a bruise. Then you turn to Jose.

> *"You must be pretty upset to hit your sister. She looks hurt – that was a pretty strong punch. Can you go and get some ice, please?"*

Now you turn to Gabriela.

> *"Is your arm really hurting? What would help – a hug?"*

You're not blaming anyone; you're just offering comfort.

When you return to speak with Jose, you give him the benefit of the doubt. Something must have upset him to punch his sister.

> *"You know how we feel about hitting in this family. I want to hear what was going on for you."*

Listen for a while, without making a judgment. The goal is to get Jose to take ownership for what happened and think about what would be more helpful than hitting next time.

"Would you like to go and see Gabriela? It would be nice for her to hear that you don't feel very good about it, too."

Most of the time, kids will go and get some ice. Most will even say they're sorry if not forced to. Forcing an apology is asking a child to deny his feelings. He should be allowed to wait until he's ready to apologize. The best way to teach our children to apologize is to be a role model and apologize to them when we have made a mistake. We are showing them that apologizing does not mean you lose face.

Other suggestions to keep in mind:

- Establish a collaborative environment at home – with less comparing and taking sides. Coach children on how to resolve conflicts before they arise.
- If your children start fighting, don't step in unless it's to mediate or stop something harmful from happening, such as when your four-year-old is about to hit her little brother over the head with a truck. Very young children need to be prevented from harming each other, but, as children grow, it is possible to reduce conflict by exploring better options at a quiet time.
- Don't take sides.

- Don't assume the youngest or weakest child is the victim. Seventy percent of fights are provoked by the younger child.
- Direct your comments at both (or all) of them, without pointing fingers.
- The right attitude is crucial. It's not just what we do, it's how we do it. If we're tense, a three-year-old will be able to see through our calm-sounding language. If we're seething in the next room, it's only a matter of time before we go crashing back in the room to take charge, all the while saying under our breath, "I knew this wouldn't work!"

It's really tempting to step in. We might even rationalize it by thinking that someone will get hurt. We might think that we have to step in to teach the kids right from wrong. Or we might just want it to end. *I can't handle it anymore!* These thoughts are understandable, but it might help to think of the big picture.

By holding back, we promote cooperation instead of rivalry. By not picking winners and losers, we also help kids learn the skills to resolve conflicts in the relative safety of the home. The more we teach conflict resolution skills and give our children the tools to defend themselves and to speak up for themselves, the better equipped they will be to handle the many social situations they will encounter when we're not there. This is a skill they'll need for the rest of their lives, and it might as well start at home.

EXERCISE: LOVING ALL YOUR CHILDREN

How to avoid two classic mistakes parents make that stoke the conflict between their kids, another gem adapted from Adele Faber and Elaine Mazlish's *Siblings Without Rivalry*:

1. Give Individually Rather Than Equally
Most parents feel a need to treat their children equally. That's a tall order and one that contributes to comparison and measuring.

> Child: *"You love her more than me!"*
>
> Instead of showing equal love (*"I love you the same as your sister"*), give individually: *"I love you 100 percent, just as you are. I couldn't love you more."*
>
> Child: *"No fair! You gave her more juice than me."*
>
> Instead of making it equal, focus on what this child wants: *"If you're still thirsty, you can help yourself to some more, too."*
>
> Child: *"Why didn't you buy me a new raincoat, too?"*
>
> Instead of making it equal, accept the child's feelings, expressing her wishes: *"You like getting new clothes, don't you? When you have outgrown your coat, we'll get you a new one, too."*

2. Describe Instead of Comparing
Instead of saying: *"Why is it that whenever I ask for help with the dishes, your brother volunteers and you always manage to disappear?"*

Describe what you need from *this* child: *"Let's talk about which night you would be willing to help with the dishes."*

Instead of saying: *"It's your own fault you have no money to buy a treat. We warned you last week to save some of your money. Your sister listened and saved half of her money."*

Acknowledge what *this* child might be feeling or wishing: *"You wish you had a treat, too. I know it can be hard to wait, but there will be another chance next weekend."*

12

Your Child Will Test You: Tools for Solving Problems – Together

Parents often ask us, "If I adopt your collaborative approach to parenting, can I discipline my child when things aren't working? How?" When they say the word *discipline*, they usually mean some form of punishment, or at least a consequence, both of which involve external motivation. There's a lingering myth that a child needs to suffer to learn. That's not what we believe. When things go off the rails, which they inevitably will, we want to provide a chance for our children to take responsibility for it, make amends, and learn from it.

Messing up is normal in any family. Kids draw on the wall, they break a Chinese vase when they're jumping off the sofa, or they might even steal money to buy candy at the store. It might be a simple mistake, something they didn't think through in advance. Or it might be intentional, repeated behavior. If it is, you can be pretty sure that something is driving this behavior and the most helpful thing we can do is figure out what it is. Then we can look for a solution with our child.

When things go wrong, we can depend on an incredibly valuable resource – our own child's natural creativity and ability to solve problems. Kids are our greatest resource. Figure them out, and they can move from resistance to cooperation. They have lots of ideas, they're creative, and they respond to problem solving.

One of the most effective lines we can use when our child has messed up is this one: "What do you think you can to do about this?" Here we are asking our child for their ideas to solve the problem, and it can transform a potentially ugly confrontation into a creative problem-solving exercise.

One of our parents came to class one day in a despondent mood. She'd been yelling at her kids all week, and she was tired and frustrated. What had happened? Her six-year-old had taken her mascara and scrawled all over the wall in the staircase, the wall in plain view of anyone sitting in the living room. She was so furious she felt like giving the child her red lipstick to finish off the job!

What was she to do? Most of us would get pretty mad at a time like this, so it may be useful to reframe the scene. Instead of seeing it as behavior that needs to be punished, you might think of it as a problem that needs to be solved. In this case, you need your child's cooperation to address the problem.

THE FIVE-STEP APPROACH TO SOLVING PROBLEMS

Here's a step-by-step problem-solving approach that may serve as a useful guide at a time like this.

1. TAKE A TIME OUT – FOR YOURSELF

When you first see the mascara, take a deep breath. And another. Go to another room for a minute if you have to. It is best not to yell. What you are doing here is showing how an adult with self-respect takes time out to manage her emotions. A yelling adult is modeling an out-of-control adult. We're not saying we'll never lose our patience and show our anger over a behavior; after all, we are human. But it is better to focus on what motivated your child to do this and how cleanup is going to be handled. Pointing out the child's carelessness or deliberateness or how bad they are will create distance between the two of you and will not solve the problem.

2. APPROACH YOUR CHILD WHEN YOU ARE CALM

When you're both calm, approach your child to start dealing with the problem. Problems can't be solved respectfully when we are stuck in "fight or flight" mode.

3. PUT YOURSELF IN YOUR CHILD'S SHOES

Say:

> *"You must have been pretty upset about something to mark up our walls like this. Do you want to tell me about it?"*

The goal here is to give your child a chance to share what was going on for her. Find out what motivated the behavior. If you have an inkling of what it could be, you can make a guess.

> *"I've been pretty busy all day getting ready for our dinner party tonight. Could it be you've been feeling ignored? Maybe a bit hurt?"*

Don't rush through this step, because it's where you win co-operation. Your child may even surprise you with a reason you never would have thought of. She may say she thought it would make the wall prettier. If the child feels you truly understand and care about her point of view, she'll participate in the rest of the problem-solving exercise without fear or resistance. Before moving on, finish with this question:

> *"Is there anything else you'd like to share with me?"*

Often children will delve into other issues that have been weighing heavily on their minds when they have a parent willing to listen. It can be a real gold mine.

4. EXPRESS YOUR FEELINGS

Keep this step brief. Say your bit in ten words or less. Otherwise you risk losing that cooperation you have just achieved.

> *"I care about you and I care about our house."*

Don't go into a rant – they've likely heard it before. Your child knows right from wrong by age five, so there's no need to lecture, either. If your child is under five, use this situation as a teaching moment and state (as calmly as possible),

> *"This isn't a respectful way to treat our home. We draw on paper, not on our walls."*

5. COLLABORATE ON A SOLUTION

So, what can we do about this mess? This is when children learn the power of brainstorming for ideas and learn that two heads are often better than one. Ideas aren't evaluated until the end. The key is to let your child share her ideas first. Since this is a pretty straightforward problem, there are only a couple of likely solutions. The child may offer to clean it up or ask us to help her clean up. She can even offer to replace Mom's mascara from her savings or allowance (another good reason to give our children allowance).

After her ideas run out, it's your turn. Some children have difficulty coming up with solutions at first, but the more practice they get with this process, the better their participation. You may give a younger child a couple of solutions to consider.

TEN IDEAS FOR RESOLVING CONFLICT

1. If you lose your temper, you'll lose your point.
2. You are trying to win an agreement, not an argument.
3. Judging your child is not necessary - generally he knows he made a mistake.
4. Apologize when you're wrong, even in minor matters.
5. Gracefully acknowledge the other's comment or statement of fact.
6. The ability to separate fact from opinion is the mark of a clear mind and reflects intellectual integrity.
7. Stay with your point; pursue your objective, but don't devastate.
8. Say what you mean and mean what you say. If you want truth, give it.
9. Bargain in good faith. Your intellect will tell you when you're bargaining, and your conscience will tell you whether or not you have good faith.
10. Don't be quick to accept a solution that you feel is too good to be true - it likely is.

Then, together with your child, choose the option you think will work best and implement it. Some issues, such as a new bedtime routine, may take a few days to solve. If so, you can say:

"I think we have a great solution here, but let's try it out for a few days and see if it's working. If not, we can always go back to the drawing board and fix it."

And if it isn't working out, it's a good idea to follow the problem-solving steps again.

These steps can be adapted to just about any situation. If you have a young child, or a simple situation, you might collapse them into one or two steps. A three-year-old child dumps his blueberry yogurt onto the kitchen floor on purpose.

We can say:

"We've got a real mess here. What do we need to do now? Can you grab the sponge and we'll do it together?"

Afterward:

"What can you do next time you don't want your food?"

A CASE IN POINT: CLEANLINESS

AN ANECDOTE FROM A PARENT

One dad in our class wanted to demonstrate to his children why cleanliness was so important. He left a dirty dinner plate on the counter for a week, long enough that a green and yucky mold established its home there. The science project became a wonderful opportunity for learning and an experience the children would never get when everything is cleaned up all the time.

It's also important to consider whether we had a role in the misbehavior. Did our child interpret our actions as disrespectful? Perhaps we ignored the child's request to get down from his chair. Or maybe when he tried to push the yogurt away, we said he had to finish it. Either of these responses can make even a three-year-old feel disrespected. So he takes matters into his own hands and pushes back or gets even.

When kids are older and the issues get more complicated and subtle, you'll find you spend more time on some of the steps of problem solving. Say your twelve-year-old son, Tony, isn't coming home in time for supper. He's always at the park with his friends, playing on his new skateboard. He seems to ignore your requests to be on time for dinner. You can use the problem-solving steps very easily in this situation:

"Tony, I've been thinking that it probably isn't easy for you to leave your friends when you are having fun. Is that right?"

"Yeah, Mom. It's not fair. All the other guys get to stay out later and I miss out on all the fun. I even missed out on a pizza night at Mark's last week 'cause of our stupid rule about family dinner."

"I'm sorry to hear this. We've got a real problem here, don't we? How about we find a better solution? Are you willing to do that with me?"

We write our ideas down.

- Tony can come home later two nights of the week and be on time the other nights.
- We can leave his dinner to stay warm in the oven those nights.
- He can use the timer on his watch to remind himself when it's time to head home.
- Dad can pick him up at the park on his way home from work.
- The family can have dinner later a couple of nights a week.
- All the kids go home at the same time.

"Tony, let's look at our list and see if there is anything we don't like. Now let's look for something we both can agree on."
"Great, let's do it for the next few nights and see how it works! If it's not quite working, we can go back to the drawing board."

This problem-solving approach has plenty of benefits for our children:

- It gives them a tool to deal with differences respectfully and a chance to strengthen their communication skills.
- They're more likely to keep agreements in which they have ownership.
- They gain self-confidence.
- They confirm that their parents' love for them is unconditional.

- Their self-esteem is never in question.
- They feel their ideas are valued.
- They learn from their mistakes.

When we've gone back to the drawing board with our child over an issue and the agreed-upon solutions are still not being respected, it may be time for what are commonly called logical consequences. We call it the *Logical Next Step.*

THE LOGICAL NEXT STEP

A young couple took their six-year-old son to a restaurant on a Saturday for what was supposed to be a fun lunch before a play date. It didn't quite work out that way. The little boy made a fuss at the restaurant, the kind of fuss that most parents dread.

After trying everything, the parents cracked down. "That's it. We are leaving. No play date for you!"

Needless to say, the little boy did not then say, "Oh Dad, now I get it and I won't make a fuss at a restaurant again."

Quite the contrary. A few minutes later, when they were driving home, the little boy started screaming at the top of his lungs. As the car was rolling down a busy street, he opened the door. Luckily, he was wearing a seat belt. His dad slammed on the brakes, closed the door, and locked it. Then his mom issued the ultimate punishment: "No TV for a week!"

Well, we'd all be distressed or furious on a day like that, but what does TV have to do with misbehaving in a restaurant or a dangerous move on the road? All behavior has a purpose.

When the little boy was acting up in the restaurant, he was trying to say something. "I'm bored," or, "I can't do this right now. The food is not coming fast enough, and I don't want to sit here anymore."

A more effective approach would be to plan ahead and be prepared for the boy's difficulty in the restaurant early on. His parents might distract him with a coloring book, or take him outside for a walk until his food arrives. If that didn't work, they could leave the restaurant. They can say calmly, "This isn't working today. It's not respectful to the other people in the restaurant, so we'd better head home." What the parent does, in other words, should relate to the child's behavior. It should make logical sense to a child. It's important to share with our children our values such as considerate behavior in public places.

This Logical Next Step works best as a last resort, when other thoughtful solutions aren't working. Here are some examples:

You see your nine-year-old riding his bike without his helmet. You have had a couple of discussions in the past and worked out an agreement that he wear his helmet. Your child is not respecting that agreement, so you decide it's time for a Logical Next Step: His bike needs to go away for a couple of days until he's prepared to respect his safety. It sounds like this:

> *"I noticed you were riding your bike without a helmet again today. Your father and I have decided it's time for you to take*

a break from biking until you are ready to be more respectful of your safety."

Your seven-year-old daughter has a friend over, and both of them tease and exclude a younger sibling. After the play date, you do some problem solving with your daughter and explore ways to improve play dates so that it's fun and respectful for all. She agrees that next time her younger sister can join in the play for a short while at the beginning. Then the older girls could have some private playtime. No teasing allowed. As well, you agree to do a separate activity with your younger daughter to keep her busy while the older girls play.

Things improve briefly, but then a play date turns chaotic. This is the time to implement a Logical Next Step. That evening, when everyone has calmed down, you speak to both girls.

"Well, that didn't work very well today, and I'm not willing to go through that again. So, we won't be inviting friends over to play for the rest of this week. We'll sit down on the weekend and see if you girls can come up with a plan to make this work better."

Your three-year-old has pushed a chair over to the counter, climbed up, and helped himself to some cookies – just before breakfast. You have a chat with him and explain:

"We eat cookies in our house as a dessert after lunch or dinner. If you'd like cookies, you can let me know, and you can

be in charge of putting them on the plate for us all to eat at dessert time."

The next week, your little boy melts down over the loss of early morning cookies. You respond calmly with all the best tools in your tool kit.

"When do we have cookies in our house?"
And, "Sounds like you wish we could have cookies all the time, but that wouldn't be good for our bodies. And I love you too much to fight over cookies, so Mommy's going to go and get your clothes ready to go to the park."

No let up. Now you decide not to put cookies on the shopping list for the next week. When your son asks for cookies before breakfast, you open the cupboard:

"The cookies are all gone."

Then you get down to your child's eye level:

"We'll get more cookies in the house when you're ready to be respectful of cookie time in our house."

You give him a hug.

"We can try again next week."

THE 3R RULE FOR LOGICAL NEXT STEPS

Whenever we feel the need to follow through on a behavior with a Logical Next Step it needs to pass this litmus test: The 3R Rule – Respectful, Reasonable, Related.

1. Be Respectful

Your tone should show respect for your child. Instead of "How dare you ..." you can say, "This isn't working today, so we need to leave."

Dreikurs put it this way: If logical consequences are used as a threat or imposed in anger, they cease being consequences and become punishments. Children are quick to discern the difference. They respond positively to logical consequences; they fight back when punished.

2. Be Reasonable

Going home when a child is acting up in a restaurant is a reasonable solution. Telling the child they won't ever come to a restaurant with you again would be unreasonable.

3. Relate the Step to the Behavior

A Logical Next Step must be related to the behavior. Leaving the restaurant passed this test. If you say to one child, "If you hit your sister, you won't have dessert," it doesn't follow. If your child talks back at the dinner table, and you say, "No TV tonight," it won't make sense. He'll only resent you for it and feel the need to retaliate.

When the Logical Next Step is used properly, it is a very effective way to respond to a child's misbehavior. Children do recognize when they are given chances but choose to disregard all efforts. They do see the fairness and they will come around.

Sometimes the Logical Next Step does not apply. If your child is attacking an important family value – by lying, for instance – he may actually be discouraged or hurting inside. In this case, it's best to focus on helping the child feel better about himself. Then better behavior will follow.

HELPFUL HINTS FOR A MORE EFFECTIVE LOGICAL NEXT STEP

- Never implement a Logical Next Step when you are upset or angry, for it ceases being respectful and becomes a punishment. Wait until you are calm.
- As you follow through, assure the child that he may try again later. Always give another chance.
- Don't be sharp. Act with love and compassion.
- State your decision once. Show faith in your child.
- Think out the logical sequence for trouble spots before approaching the child. Does it pass the 3R litmus test?
- Ask yourself, "Why do I want to change my child's behavior?" Clarify values.
- Form house rules together – the fewer, the better. Think about making a collaborative agreement where the needs of the situation rule.

A CASE IN POINT: STEALING

One of the more upsetting moments as a parent comes when you learn that your child has stolen something. You may see it as a personal affront that your child could have done something so wrong. You feel hurt, and you may think something like this: *Where did I go wrong? How did I fail this child?* or, *What did I do to deserve this kind of behavior?* You might also slip right into fear for the future and think, *This is it, my child is headed for a life of crime!*

However, it is common for most children to take something that does not belong to them at some point. Although you might be hurt and distressed, you should handle this situation calmly and respectfully, as you would any other mistake.

Stealing (or nonchalantly putting things in one's pocket and forgetting) is a common behavior in children. If you show anger or punish them, you run the risk of retaliation, and the child will just be more careful not to get caught next time. This problem is best resolved with compassion and kindness for the child (this does not imply acceptance of the misbehavior). Showing that you love and believe in your child goes a long way toward confirming his sense of worth.

Look for a solution together. If the behavior repeats itself, it moves from a mistake in judgment to a problem that needs to be addressed. It is important for parents not to overreact, punish, or dole out unrelated consequences. These reactions only make the situation worse.

The best course of action depends on the age of the child. Children up to age three or four take things simply because they want them. They typically think about themselves before others. Just state that they must return the item and ask how they would feel if someone took something of theirs. A supportive tone of voice will encourage your child to respond in the way you hope. This way, you're creating a teachable moment by showing kindness toward your child, at the same time showing them a way to make amends and be respectful of others.

Older children are likely to steal for more serious reasons. It's important that parents look for the motivation behind the theft. A common reason is to retaliate. When a child feels hurt, not cared about, or misunderstood, she feels justified in getting even or hurting back.

If you suspect your child is stealing but you don't have proof, it is important not to put him in a position where he feels forced to lie by accusing him. If you accuse your child and he denies it, you need to show him trust and apologize. If you accuse your child wrongly, it will hurt him even more and can cause distance in the relationship. In this case, it's better to say:

> *"I am missing three twenty-dollar bills. Could it be that you took them and are afraid to tell me? I won't be mad at you either way. If you need more money, we can talk about that."*

If he does not confess, express your faith in him and drop the issue. If he does confess, keep your word. Do not get angry or punish him. Otherwise, your child will lose trust in you and perhaps start lying to protect himself in the future. Our goal is to understand what motivated our child to take the money and resolve that.

If you are not sure who took the money, you could mention to the whole family that it is missing from your purse and that you would like it back, anonymously. Emphasize your faith in your children and how you would like to help them get what they want in the proper way. If the money is returned, thank your children for their honesty and leave it at that. If the money is not returned, you might initiate a discussion. Talk about alternatives to stealing and help your children explore how they can get the things they want or need through jobs or their allowance. Although it is counterintuitive, do not insist on finding out who took the money. It is better to drop the issue and keep your wallet out of sight for the time being.

If you catch your child stealing from you or from someone else, remember that anger and punishment are not the solution. State that what he did is wrong and he must return the object or pay for it. Acknowledge that this is difficult and embarrassing, and consider accompanying him for support. You might share a similar incident in your own childhood. Mention that everyone makes mistakes, and they can be rectified. Emphasize that although what your child did was unacceptable, you still believe in him and love him.

APPLY THE FIVE STEP PROBLEM-SOLVING APPROACH

1. Take a time out – for yourself.

2. Approach your child when you are calm.

3. Put yourself in your child's shoes.

See the problem from their perspective.

> *"I know this is uncomfortable for you so I appreciate you sitting to talk. I gather you took my money because you felt you needed something pretty badly."*

Your child might say:

> *"Yes, all my friends get way more allowance than me. They get to buy themselves cool things and go to movies and stuff. I've asked you so many times about my allowance and you keep saying when I'm older. You never listen. I want to get some new Warhammer figures, and it will take me months to save with the money I get."*

4. Express your feelings (in ten words or less).

"I'm sorry it hurt you when I didn't listen."

5. Collaborate on a solution.

"Let's see how we can solve this problem. Why don't you share your ideas first?"

Some ideas:

1. Do a budget and look at his needs.
2. Consider increasing his allowance.

3. Make a list of extra jobs (over and above his regular chores) that he could be paid to do.
4. Research jobs in the community he could do – dog walking, paper delivering, lawn cutting.
5. Open a bank account so he can save more easily.

Agree on some solutions together and try them out for a couple of weeks. While the answer is not to give our children everything their friends have, making a plan gives them a sense of control and teaches them more effective and respectful ways to solve problems. Check in again and tweak the plan if necessary. If it's working, congratulate yourselves on a job well done.

Lying and dishonesty are other challenges parents can face. To discourage these, we have to model honest behavior. If we are pleased to receive more change than we are due, if we allow our child to lie about his age to save money at the theatre, or if we sneak supplies home from work or restaurants, we're sending the wrong message to our kids. We must also respect other people's rights and personal property, and not show distrust by rifling through our children's rooms or backpacks without their permission. We can make a point of being honest even when no one is looking. That teaches children the value of honesty.

In the crunch, when our kids mess up, it's important to change our negative thoughts about what might happen in the future. This won't solve the problem, and it only increases our anxiety and frustration. Instead, it's better to replace the

Discipline:
To teach or train another person.

negative thoughts about our child with more constructive ones: *I love my child, but I don't love what he is doing at the moment! This is a good time to teach my child about respect.*

This, too, will pass. Just have some faith.

PUNITIVE TIME OUT VS RESPECTFUL TIME OUT

PUNITIVE TIME OUTS

Time out has become a popular method of discipline for young children. Most parenting books talk about removing a misbehaving child from the situation until she calms down and is ready to behave better. Unfortunately, time out is often imposed in a punitive manner or with a harsh tone of voice.

> *"Go to your room this instant and think about what you've done and don't come out until I tell you to."*
> *Or, "Sit on that stair, young lady, until you are ready to apologize!"*

In many schools, time out means segregation or sitting in the principal's office. The public humiliation is supposed to teach the child a lesson. Yet the tactic usually backfires.

Punitive time out may stop the behavior in the short term, but it does nothing to address the reason for the behavior or help a child develop long-term goals, like self-control, respect in relationships, better behavior, and high self-esteem. During time out, a child may feel hurt and resentful. *This is unfair. My parents are mean.* She might start to look down on herself. *I'm a bad person.* This is not the kind of remorse parents might expect!

Some kids might escalate and start plotting revenge. *I'll get even with my sister for telling on me.* Or they might plot a future rebellion. *I'll do just the opposite to prove that Dad's not the boss of me.* Or they get sneaky. *I won't get caught next time.*

That's not the end of the trouble with time out, either. Some kids can't stay put during time out. Others trash their room, or withdraw.

Long-term, time out doesn't work if it's delivered in a punitive way. It's supposed to make a child pay for what he has done, but it doesn't help him learn how to avoid doing it again. It's based on the notion that to make a child do better, we need to make him feel worse. It shames a child and deprives him of dignity and respect. This doesn't work for anyone.

RESPECTFUL TIME OUTS

Jane Nelsen in her book *Positive Time Out* discusses seeing time outs instead as flowing from the simple, yet groundbreaking idea that children "do better when they feel better." If a child is having trouble, respectful time out gives him a break from the situation or from other people until he feels better. It's based on the idea that children do better when they feel better.

Respectful time out gives children a chance to learn how to manage their emotions and control their behavior.

We learn from experience what type of time out works best for a particular child. Is it talking through the problem with a calm, caring adult? Getting a hug? Jumping on the trampoline or doing twenty somersaults? Maybe it's the child going to their special place for solace. We feel this makes more sense than the punitive version. Put yourself in the child's position. As a parent, what type of a time out would you like when you're feeling irritable, tired, or moody? Sitting on a hard step and feeling ashamed, or having a cup of tea and curling up in bed with a good book? Or, better still, finding someone caring to be with you?

INVOLVE CHILDREN IN THE CREATION OF THEIR SPECIAL PLACE

Set it up:

> *"You know how Mom and Dad sometimes leave the room and take deep breaths so we won't yell? Where could you go to do that? Would you feel better if you had a place to calm down when you needed it?"*

Get the children involved in the planning and naming of the place: a cushion fort in the corner of the playroom, their own bedroom, perhaps a couch. Have children come up with a name for their place – Taro's Crash Pad, Alia's Special Place, Pillow Pocket. Ask them to supply it with what they need – blanket, music player, books, snacks.

Practice with younger children. On a day that they're feeling good, you can go with them to the special place. Young children love to role-play!

Here's a tip you could try: When a problem arises, let the child choose time out for himself. If he doesn't, perhaps say:

"Would it help you feel better to go to your Crash Pad for a few minutes? Would you prefer if I went with you? Well, you may not want to go, but I think I will go to mine. I think it will help me calm down."

After time out, help the child explore the benefits of making amends. Brainstorm how to fix the problem, try again, and help someone the child may have hurt feel better.

Respectful time out has plenty of advantages:

- It gives children confidence that things can get better.
- It gives them a chance to regroup without losing face.
- It's respectful – children are involved participants.
- They can learn from their mistakes and make amends.
- It promotes self-soothing and self-control.

LOGICAL NEXT STEP VS. PUNISHMENT

As we have seen, punishment does not help our children learn positive behavior. This chart shows how punishment differs from the Logical Next Step, and shows how we can put ourselves on the right path of respectfully guiding our children and encouraging their internal motivation.

Logical Next Step	**Punishment**
1. A learning process – encourages the love of exploring and being creative • Respectful of the child • Separates the deed from the doer • Child is accepted although his behavior is not; unconditional love is involved	1. End result success/failure process – creates the fear of failure and disapproval • Belittles child • Equates the deed with the doer • Child is rejected; conditional love is involved
2. Related logically to the behavior (i.e., "I believe you can learn to make responsible choices") • Reasonable and seen as fair – invites cooperation and collaboration • Child has a choice regarding his behavior and the results (i.e., "Use your judgment.") • Parent expresses confidence in the child's ability to handle mistakes and failures	2. An arbitrary connection between behavior and its punishment. (i.e., "I'll teach you a lesson. You deserve what you are getting") • Often seen as unfair – invites hurt and retaliation • No choice for the child (i.e., "You can't be trusted to make good judgments") • Parent has no confidence in the child's ability to handle mistakes and failures
Adult is: • An educator • Understanding and empathetic • Respectful of the child and her abilities • Expressing that the child is always worthy • Interested in a learning situation	Adult is: • A judge, jury and executioner • Disapproving and angry • Fearful for/discouraged about the child • Expressing that the child is sometimes unworthy • Interested only in success

A SUMMARY OF HOW TO USE THE LOGICAL NEXT STEP:

1. Always implement with an attitude of LRB – love, respect and belief
2. Clarify values: "Why do I want to change my child's behavior?"
3. Always give another chance. This is a learning process – assure your child that he may try again later.
4. If the challenging behavior is repeated, extend the time that must elapse before the child gets another chance.

A CASE IN POINT

A PARENT'S TEMPER TANTRUM BREAKTHROUGH

We have been making more effort not to fight with and not to give in to our determined six-year-old daughter, Sarah, who has a history of being demanding and bossy with us.

She doesn't like this one little bit. She had a five-star Texas chili temper tantrum this weekend, which we haven't seen in a long time. Someone in her class can do cursive letters, and she wanted me to do her Valentines with cursive writing for her. I said no, that wouldn't be honest. I was willing to write the letters on a piece of paper for her to copy, if she would like.

She got more and more upset and cranky and started tearing up her craft paper. I suggested she might go upstairs and calm down and come back when she was feeling better. She went ballistic. She was screaming and crying. She went to her room and carried on up there with the hope that we would give in – as we often did in the past!

We decided to give her some time and space, so we ignored the situation and didn't respond in any way to her. At one point we heard her yelling upstairs, "I don't like it when you ignore meee!" She escalated and finally collapsed in her room.

At that point I went up with a cool cloth and gently wiped her face, gave her a hug, and told her I loved her.

She is in complete shock at our change in reaction. I think we are on our way to more dual respect in our relationship.

INVITING COOPERATION

Sometimes children are not even close to having a tantrum; they just don't like being manipulated. For example, Doone tells a story about her son Alec, when he was about five. Alec was told to smile for his baseball photograph and the photographer made all kinds of faces to get him to cooperate. When a very serious photo was the result and Alec was asked why he didn't smile, he answered, "The guy wasn't funny enough!" We are sure a simple "please" or an explanation would have done the trick.

EXERCISE: APPROACHES THAT INVITE COOPERATION

It's time to put it all together and put it into practice.

In the first situation, a grocery store showdown, we provide some suggestions. Then you can select a recent situation you found challenging and write down responses that might have been more helpful for next time. That's one thing we can count on with children ... there will always be a next time!

1. Give information.
"It's not respectful to other shoppers when you run in the aisles."

2. Redirect.
"Tell Mom what you would like to do this weekend with the family."

3. Ask for help.
"It would be helpful if you picked out four apples for us."

4. Give the child a way to contribute.
"This is your list of groceries to put in the cart."

5. Give choices.
"Which would you prefer, to walk next to me or sit in the cart?"

6. Take action (if child disregards choice).
"I am sorry to have to pick you up, but this isn't

working." Calmly place the child in the cart. If it's an older child, ask # 7 below.

7. Problem solve (ahead of time when possible).
"What can we do so that it works out better in the store today?"

8. Encourage.
"I enjoyed having you with me – let's do it again."

9. Don't fight or give in.
"This isn't working today, so we have to leave. We'll try again another day."

Reflect on a recent situation of your own and fill in the tools that you feel would be useful for next time:

1. Give information.

2. Redirect.

3. Ask for help.

4. Give the child a way to contribute.

5. Give choices.

6. Take action (if child disregards choice).

7. Problem solve (ahead of time when possible).

8. Encourage.

9. Don't fight or give in.

What to Do When: Putting Your Problem-Solving Tools into Practice

We close this book with situations that may well loom on your horizon as a parent. However, we believe the tools we've discussed in this book make you more than ready for them. Take a look at how we suggest you apply them.

1. HARRY WON'T DO HIS HOMEWORK!

Why do kids have homework, anyway? The purpose of homework for children who are twelve and under is to get them comfortable with managing their learning at home. It helps them to take a step toward long-term goals, like independence, time management, and having a good work ethic. The aim is for them to get into the habit of sitting in a quiet space and focusing on something by themselves. At the same time, we want to incorporate the belief that exploring, being curious, and learning are enjoyable.

The parent's role is to set their child up for independent learning at home, get them started, and then get out of the way. Once kids get into their homework, we can act as coaches and consultants, but the idea is to work ourselves out of this job.

Of course, it doesn't always happen this way. Some kids take time to learn these skills. They may not want to do their homework, not tonight or ever, and this can easily launch a parent into punishment mode. "No TV for you tonight!"

We all want to avoid these kinds of fights with our kids, so it's wise to address both the practical and fundamental issues.

First, the practical issues:

- Make sure your child has the physical space and support he needs. Set up a corner with an appropriately sized chair and table, ample lighting, and minimal distractions. Some children do better in their own rooms and some do better in the hub of the house, in the kitchen or family room. When you're not sure what's best, ask your child what they would prefer. Test it out and see what works.
- Have plenty of supplies – paper, pencils, pens, a dictionary – on hand. Help your child organize this space with folders, shelves, and labels. How you keep your home office is a good role-modeling opportunity.
- Create a routine after school. A snack, some exercise, and some rest or social time are all very important for children, especially after they have been at school all

day. Try to schedule your own work or reading at the same time.

- Create some agreements about when and how much screen time. Involve your child in the decision and the schedule. The schedule can vary according to his extracurricular activities and the timing of his favorite shows. You might agree that he can watch some TV before doing his work and set a time limit beforehand.
- Act as a helper, guide, resource person, or coach, but don't actually do your child's homework. That can lead to major problems down the road. She becomes dependent on you and doesn't learn to do the work for herself. Not only that, but the teacher gets a false impression of your child's understanding of the work.
- Recognize different learning styles. Some children multitask. Some need to move as they learn. Some kids might want to sit on a bouncy ball; others may prefer to lie on the floor. Some listen to music; others need silence. It may be helpful to schedule lots of breaks on a homework night. Working with friends can make all the difference.
- Some kids refuse to do homework because they're worried about performance or looking inadequate. Let this kind of child know that mistakes are okay. They are part of being human and even welcome in the learning process. They point to gaps in knowledge that need to

be filled. Don't insist on perfection or make your child do it over; this is the teacher's job.

- Don't even make your child finish. If he puts in a good solid effort and runs out of time, it's an important indicator for his teacher of how much he is capable of. Maybe it's an indicator that he doesn't fully understand the concepts.
- In the long run, scolding and nagging won't help. Maintaining a calm, peaceful relationship with an attitude of confidence in your child is much more effective.

These are the practical issues, but Harry's reluctance to do homework may point to a more fundamental issue. Many children have not yet discovered the joy of learning. They might feel that homework is an onerous chore, especially when there's so much competition for their attention from games, TV, and friends. How do we make learning a pleasure from a very early age? We have to show that we, as parents, don't know everything, either, and that we love learning, too. It may not be an easy task for some people to admit that they don't know something. It might feel like a sign of weakness and inferiority, something to avoid. If this is the case, we have to overcome this feeling in order to enjoy learning and pass that on to our kids. Even when we stumble as we learn, our worthiness is never in question. With practice we can learn that being less knowledgeable is a welcome and enjoyable opportunity to explore and learn.

But what if your ten-year-old son just won't do his homework? Here's an approach that works well for many of the parents we coach:

First, sit down with your son at a quiet time when neither of you are stressed – not, for example, when it's 8 p.m. and he's been playing games instead of doing his homework. Then empathize:

"I can see you're having trouble focusing on your homework. What's going on?"

Listen to him as he complains about the teacher, the stupid homework, and how he'd rather be doing something else. You could say:

"I don't want to fight with you about it. I want to help you. How can we make this work better?"

He might come up with a fine solution – like getting up early to do his homework so he can watch a favorite show later. Give it a try; he might make it work. If it doesn't work, say:

"I won't protect you from the results of your choice. If you haven't done your homework, you can take it up with your teacher."

Book a talk with the teacher so that your child can explain to his teacher why he doesn't like homework. That conversation may produce a solution.

2. SONJA WON'T DO THE DISHES EVEN THOUGH IT'S HER JOB!

It's good for kids to do jobs around the house, learn to do things for others, and feel that they are making a contribution to the family. Being involved in the flow of family life brings children closer to the long-term goals of community-mindedness, independence, and being a good roommate one day. But often kids look at jobs as a pain and have other things they prefer to do – such as watch TV, text their friends, or play with their siblings. We do the jobs for them, feeling pretty resentful about it.

This is a time for a problem-solving session with your child, or with the whole family if the situation involves everyone. You might kick off the topic by saying:

> *"I'm not willing to do everything. We all have to share and contribute. These are the jobs that need to be done. What do you think you would like to do: Meals? Dishes? Are there other jobs you'd like to see on the list? Do you want to try something for a week and then switch jobs? Can we have a schedule? What's the best way to do this?"*

The key to success with jobs is to have the children commit to a time when the job will be done. When it's time for the dishes to be washed, don't be surprised to hear the dishwasher-in-chief say:

"Mom, a show's starting I want to watch. Can I do the dishes later?"

This is just the kind of scenario that can raise any parent's blood pressure, but it's important not to react. Instead, empathize.

"There may be a show starting ..."

State calmly what was agreed to.

"... but we agreed dishes would be done right after dinner."

Be supportive.

"If you hurry, you won't miss too much of the show."

Another option, based on the needs of the situation:

"If the show is that important, would you like to swap and do dishes for me tomorrow night?"

It really helps to give kids a say over the type of jobs they'll do at home. One parent we know had a ten-year-old son who was a whiz on the computer. He offered to map out the route for the family car trip to Florida. He even researched hotels and motels where the family could stay along the way. Contributing gives a child a sense of belonging, a sense that he or she is valuable to the family.

Sometimes children resist chores no matter what you do. This can be caused by deeper, more complex issues. If a child is being difficult and uncooperative in many areas of family life, it may be because she feels dictated to or discouraged. For this kind of child, it's best to encourage participation bit by bit. She wants to make a fruit salad on Saturday? That's a start, and you can build on that success so she feels the joy of contributing. She may start saying to herself, *In my little way, I'm valued here.*

You might hear complaints from the other kids. "Why am I doing more than she is? It's not fair." You can tell them, "When she's feeling happier or better about things, she'll be more cooperative."

MAGIC BULLET
Love Leads to Performance

In the traditional controlling approach to family relationships, a person had to perform in order to obtain love and approval. In the guiding, collaborative approach, love and approval are given first and performance happily follows.

Sometimes it takes a while for a person to believe they are cared about no matter what. Their behavior will be slow to change, but stay the course and they'll come around when they feel safe and sure.

3. SCREEN TIME IS OUT OF CONTROL!

Most of the parents we know face this issue. How do you manage screen time given the profusion of screens, big and small, that are so close at hand? Or do you even try?

It's another time for family problem solving. Your family can decide together how much screen time is appropriate, where, and when. A good place to begin is to clarify your values. Whatever schedule you come up with needs to include time for healthful activities, such as sports or fitness, quality sleep, homework, and other interests.

Screens are a privilege, and this is a chance to let your children show they can handle the responsibility. If you give them a chance, they'll love the ownership and the opportunity to show that they can make it work.

4. MY CHILD SAYS SHE'S BEING BULLIED.

This is a painful thing to hear. It's so easy to jump into protective mode to save our kids from harm and suffering. Yet this is the very time we need to be clear about our goals. There are three things to focus on:

1. How serious the situation is. What happened?
2. Whether or not your child had a role in the problem or contributed to the situation somehow.

3. What tools are available for her to deal with the problem herself.

If you hear this complaint, start out by listening.

"What happened? How do you feel about it? What did you think about yourself and the situation?"

Don't discount your child's story or suggest she somehow deserved the bad treatment. Empathize with your child.

"It sounds like you were pretty hurt when the other girls laughed at your new coat and called you a blimp."

This is a good time to share with your child the importance of deciding for herself how she feels about her new coat. You can talk with her about how to show self-respect. You can also talk about whether she wants to stay hurt by the comments. We may feel hurt initially, but we can make a choice to not stay hurt and not succumb to other people's approval. This can be a challenge even for us adults!

Next, ask your child to think of what she can do, what actions she'd like to take.

"How do you think you'd like to handle this?"

You can explore with your child the tools, words, and strategies to use if the girls say something unkind again. For instance, tell the girl how those words make you feel. Disengage and go somewhere else. Find someone else to be with.

If the bullying persists, you and your child can go to the teacher and work together to resolve the issue. That usually is enough. Most bullying issues can be resolved at the grassroots level.

5. MY CHILD WON'T GO TO BED ON TIME!

Bedtime can easily turn into a battle, especially if parents try to control their child, but it doesn't have to be that way.

It might help to remember that you cannot force a child to sleep, so there's not much point in dictating a fall-asleep time. As our children get older, we want them to listen to the needs of their own body and start taking more charge of themselves. When it's bedtime, you can say:

> *"Okay, we're finished with stories and hugs. It's time to say goodnight. Would you like me to turn out the light, or do you want to do that for yourself?"*

If your child chooses to look at books a little longer, or play quietly on their bed, you can see how he handles it.

An older child might stay up past his normal sleep time, just to show he can, but he'll be slumbering on the desk in math class the next day. Most kids don't like feeling tired throughout the day. If they are given a choice regarding their bedtime, chances are that, after a while, they'll choose a more appropriate time to go to sleep. Many of our skeptical parents reported that after a couple of days, they heard these magical words from their child:

"Dad, I'm tired. I think I'll head up to bed."

One of our goals is to let go so that our children can learn from their choices, and this is an ideal place to do it. It's not a life or death issue. It doesn't put our child at risk to nod off in class or feel crummy during sports practice.

It's important to be flexible about bedtime, especially in the summer. One of our parents came to class one summer day. She was having a real problem.

"I'm having arguments with my kids every night when I try to get them in the house. Bedtime has become World War III around here," she complained. "The evenings are bright and many of the neighbors' kids are out late, but my children are only eight and ten years old and still need to get to bed at a reasonable time. Help!"

Routines are vital for family harmony, and they teach children great things such as self-discipline and respect for order. However, a change of seasons usually involves a change in routine, and we need to be flexible. Summer, after all, is different. It stays brighter outside, and there's no school in the morning. Streets are full of noise and activity. We all remember the thrill of summer holidays when we were kids. We also probably remember giving our own parents a hard time at bedtime. So to break that pattern and make our own families run more smoothly, we need to get our children on board and cooperate with them.

The best place to start is with a collaborative problem-solving exercise:

"We're having some challenges getting to bed on time and I'd like to hear your ideas to make our evenings and bedtime work better."

Agree on a meeting time that suits everyone. Start the discussion off by acknowledging your children's position first.

"You're having fun outside with the kids on the street, and you don't think it's fair that you have to come in soooo early. Is that how you see it?"

Give the children a chance to talk about the injustice of it all. Listen without comment; just saying, "Mmm" or phrases like "I see" can help. Then summarize what you've heard them say.

"So you feel that we should relax the rules because it's summer, and you believe you can handle a later bedtime. Is that correct? Anything else?"

Now it's time to share your point of view. Keep this brief since they've heard you rant and rave for days now.

"I love you too much to fight every night."

"Let's not argue about it every night."

"I want to end our days on a happy note."

Now, brainstorm to come up with a better evening routine for the family. Everyone can present ideas, even crazy ones. At this stage, all ideas are accepted. It's a good idea to jot them down. Also, you want to keep the process positive. This isn't the time to evaluate or knock ideas.

Then you can sort through the suggestions to create a solution. The process of elimination can work well. The goal is to agree on a solution that's mutually satisfactory. Get them to write down the revised routine and agree to test it out for a few nights to see if it works for everyone. Make sure you schedule a time to chat about how it's going after the few nights. Follow-through is key to the success of these sorts of agreements. If it's working, congratulate yourselves; if it isn't, go back to the drawing board.

Ideas in case you get stuck:

1. Change dinner hour to allow for longer outdoor time (even if for only two nights per week).
2. Simplify dinners – try sandwiches with veggies and dip.
3. Place a blanket on the lawn and have an outdoor picnic.
4. Do story time earlier in the day (when it's too hot to be outdoors) to allow more playtime in the evening.
5. Instead of a bath, have the children run through the sprinkler before bed.
6. Coordinate outdoor time with the neighbors.

With any luck, some of these ideas will stop World War III in its tracks.

6. MY CHILD INTERRUPTS ME WHEN I'M AT DINNER WITH FRIENDS!

A dad in one of our classes shared this success story:

> I had a great experience with the kids when we had company for dinner and my seven-year-old daughter had a girlfriend for a sleepover as well.
>
> At eight thirty, I said goodnight to them and went downstairs to be with our friends. As I expected, it wasn't long before the girls were in the dining room asking to be tucked in. I had prepared our company for this. We handled the situation as discussed in the last class.
>
> We said, "It's our time now," and continued our conversation with our friends.
>
> Everyone acted as if the girls weren't there. It worked! They hung around for a few minutes and finally left. I thought for sure they would be back, but they weren't.
>
> The fun part is that we later found all these notes on the stairs going up to their room. They said, "Dear Dad, we can't sleep." Another said, "No" and had two sad faces. When we got upstairs, there they were, sound asleep in bed.

I couldn't believe it. It worked. It's the first time I haven't had to tuck her in more than once.

Here are a few tips to help you enjoy dinner with friends without interruptions:

1. Preview: Discuss the plan for the evening with your children ahead of time. Agree on the time when you will say goodnight and no longer be available. Let them plan what they would like to do while you visit with your company. They could play some board games or make some popcorn and put on a movie.
2. Give them a way to participate: Children like to meet and interact with their parents' friends. Let them pass around the appetizers or greet people at the door.
3. Clue in your guests: If you think your children may test the limits, prepare your guests for how you plan to deal with the situation, so that you are more relaxed and comfortable.
4. Logical Next Step: Plan ahead how you might deal with any testing from your child, and follow through. Remember that this is an opportunity to show your child that, no matter what, you are going to respect yourself.

THE CASE FOR CHILDREN CONTRIBUTING AROUND THE HOME

If you think that getting your child to take on more tasks and jobs around the home is going to free up lots of your time, you might be disappointed. In time perhaps it will, but in the short run it will take a big investment in energy and time from you, the parent. We believe it's worth it. Other than for the obvious benefit of skill development, having children pitch in fosters the attitude of caring and sharing in life.

When kids pitch in, they learn:

- The value of teamwork
- How to live and work cooperatively with others
- The importance of follow-through on agreements
- Independence and self-respect
- To feel able and confident
- To respect others and the needs of the situation
- The joys of contribution and doing for others
- The courage to embrace new or challenging tasks
- How to use their creativity
- The resilience to bounce back from disappointments when things don't work out

How we can do this? Create a cooperative atmosphere:

- Let children choose jobs they'd like to do.
- Tasks should be within reach of the child's abilities.
- Have the kids make a chart or list of the jobs chosen – who does what and when.

- Give feedback; acknowledge child's effort.
- Don't criticize poor results. Steer toward improvement.
- Show confidence in the child.

Confidence boosters:

- *"Let's do this together so it goes faster. We all can contribute."*
- *"You try. You're able to learn."*
- *"You can do it. You're capable."*
- *"Thank you. It really helps when everyone pitches in."*
- *"What would happen if you added half a cup? Try to figure it out."*

Conclusion

Congratulations! What a journey we have been on together! By reading this book, you have made an important commitment to your parenting and your children. There have been goals to set, self-awareness to develop, reflexes to understand, improved attitudes to absorb, and new patterns of behavior to learn.

The parenting journey is different for each of us. Some parents embrace improvement and change with ease while others find the process slow and sometimes painful. Wherever you find yourself in this spectrum, please continue to encourage yourself, acknowledge your efforts, learn from any setbacks, and move forward.

We hope this book has made life easier for you and your families and will continue to do so. We hope you will get more joy from one of your most important jobs, raising great kids. The principles and techniques that we have shared are not surprising when you consider that children are really just small people. They have the same needs as adults – unconditional love, respect, and belief in themselves. These are basic human needs and necessary for every person's emotional health.

You may have found some of the ideas surprising, such as not punishing misbehavior or not saying "great job." But continue to give them a try and see how your children respond. We think you'll be amazed. While it may feel forced at the beginning, it will become second nature as you practice.

Then, as you become comfortable with these new approaches and words, you'll notice an improvement in your children's behavior. Their reactions will encourage you to continue in this new way, and you will be happily lifted in an upward spiral. We promise that this new way of parenting will get easier with time. It will be well worth all the effort.

We listen to people we like and respect, and so do our kids. By being more respectful to our children, we have a much better chance of maintaining our influence as they grow. Paradoxically, by focusing less on control and more on the relationship, we actually increase the likelihood of our children taking our advice.

You'll see the biggest benefit when your children become adolescents and teenagers. Both you and your children will be prepared for almost anything the teen years may bring. You will have a template for handling the logical next step, problem solving, power struggle issues, sibling rivalry, and many other issues.

Your teenagers will be more independent, respectful, confident, responsible, and empathetic. You will have encouraged them to achieve all the long-term goals you set out at the beginning of this journey. What's more, when your teens feel loved and not judged, when they feel respected and valued, they will be less likely to seek out high-risk behaviors. They won't need them. They will rebel less and be able to resist peer pressure more. They won't feel as entitled or be as dependent as many teens are today. They will have weathered many storms and rainy days and be more prepared for life.

Parents have told us they not only notice changes in their families as a result of the principles in this book and our teaching but in their adult relationships as well. When they apply their learning to spouses, in-laws, grandparents, colleagues, and friends, everybody benefits. Self-respect is practiced, boundaries are set, problems are resolved more calmly, and yelling and fighting are diminished. As more than one parent has exclaimed, "It's a miracle!"

We are thrilled that you have joined us on this journey of raising great parents. The journey continues. We invite you to share your stories with us at our website, www.parentingnetwork.ca.

Doone and Beverley

Your Parenting Approach: A Post-Quiz

It's time for you to fill out the first exercise again now that you have completed this book. This is a chance for you to see the progress you have made and the new skills you have learned – a chance to celebrate your improvement.

First, circle how you would rate yourself in the third column.

Second, go back to the pre-quiz at the beginning of this book and transfer your scores from there to the second column here.

Third, compare where you are now with where you were then.

We suggest you come back to this page from time to time to check your ongoing progress as you continue to sharpen your skills on your journey to being a great parent.

AS A PARENT, I ...	YOUR PRE-QUIZ RATING	YOUR POST-QUIZ RATING
Have fun and positive times with my child(ren)	No Sometimes Often Usually	No Sometimes Often Usually
Have a lot of worry and fear when it comes to parenting	No Sometimes Often Usually	No Sometimes Often Usually
Give my child(ren) a voice and say in decisions	No Sometimes Often Usually	No Sometimes Often Usually
Raise my voice or yell to be heard	No Sometimes Often Usually	No Sometimes Often Usually
Have provided my child(ren) with regular jobs to do in the home	No Sometimes Often Usually	No Sometimes Often Usually
Argue with my child(ren)	No Sometimes Often Usually	No Sometimes Often Usually
Am comfortable with my child(ren) making mistakes or struggling	No Sometimes Often Usually	No Sometimes Often Usually
Understand the reasons behind a child's misbehavior	No Sometimes Often Usually	No Sometimes Often Usually
Use bribery, threats, or remove privileges when my child(ren) don't cooperate	No Sometimes Often Usually	No Sometimes Often Usually

Take time outs for me until I calm down	No Sometimes Often Usually	No Sometimes Often Usually
Use consequences to discipline my child(ren)	No Sometimes Often Usually	No Sometimes Often Usually
Love my child(ren) no matter how they behave	No Sometimes Often Usually	No Sometimes Often Usually
Apologize to my child(ren) when I make a mistake	No Sometimes Often Usually	No Sometimes Often Usually
Have worked out morning and bedtime routines with my child(ren)	No Sometimes Often Usually	No Sometimes Often Usually
See my child(ren) as able to handle their daily life	No Sometimes Often Usually	No Sometimes Often Usually
Look for ways to improve life skills that my child(ren) will need for their future	No Sometimes Often Usually	No Sometimes Often Usually
Am on the same parenting page as my partner	No Sometimes Often Usually	No Sometimes Often Usually

Acknowledgements

One of the great aspects of our Adlerian community is its spirit of giving and sharing. We have grown much richer in knowledge as a result. A difficulty that can arise from such a sharing community is tracking down the original source of a great idea or exercise. We have endeavored to acknowledge the originator of the many gems we share with you in our book. If we have inadvertently missed anyone, we apologize.

We would like to acknowledge the following colleagues and brilliant teachers in our community: Marion Balla, Betty Lou Bettner, Dan and Marilyn Dalton, Linda Jessup, Amy Lew, Lynn Lott, Jody McVittie, Edna Nash, Jane Nelsen, Linda Page, Althea Poulos, Alyson Schafer, Stan Shapiro, and Frank and Kathleen Walton.

Personal acknowledgements from Beverley:

A few colleagues have been a particularly vital part of my journey. Lori Ulmer and Rochelle Diamond, it was a joy to share the adventure of becoming parent educators together and cheer each other on during those early years. I think you would agree that Marty and Georgine Nash were our guiding lights through it all.

My thanks as well ...

To several encouraging friends: Pam Bingham, Catherine Clark, Holly Robertson, and Andrea Senecal.

To the many parents who have become my friends over the years – you put your trust in me, invited me into your homes, and always encouraged me to capture our wonderful ideas in a book for parents everywhere: Elizabeth and Brian Brittain, Gill Deacon, Gillian Irving, Joy Morassutti, Pauline Thompson, and Emma Waverman.

To my children, Kate, Andrew, Gillian, and Madeline, who inspire me to do my best: Thank you for the joy you bring to my life. Thank you to my husband, for believing in me and for embracing the parenting philosophy that would gradually transform our family life. I am blessed to have your wisdom and love.

Personal acknowledgements from Doone:

I would like to thank the many colleagues and friends who provided advice and support over the past ten years and more.

Cathy Clark, Jane and Ron Lalonde, Sue Matthews, Susan Meech, Maria and Frank Techar, Don Tapscott, Lyn Whitham, and Lynda and Ian Wookey all made suggestions and provided encouragement.

Thank you to my children, Eric, Morgan, Alexander, and Madison, who bring out the best in me and allow me to bring out the best in them. Thank you to my husband, George, the love of my life.

Personal acknowledgements from Martin:

There are many people I wish to thank, both in the Adlerian community and the scientific circles I have been exposed to. I am especially grateful to Edith and Milton Dewey, who introduced Dr. Dreikurs' concepts to Toronto, and to Dr. Harold Mosak, Dr. Robert Powers, Dr. Kurt Adler, and Dr. Eva Dreikurs, who devoted their time and energy to educate us in Toronto.

I am particularly thankful to my wife, Georgine, with whom I developed many of the ideas in this book. I also learned so much about human behavior from my sons, Richard, Stephen, and Eric, who provided many occasions for practical experience.

* * *

A terrific team helped us get our book to the finish line. We thank Stan Behal, our wonderful portrait photographer. We thank Don Bastian, Deirdre Walters, Ann Westlake, and Sarah Scott for providing invaluable writing and editing contributions and for guiding us – patiently – along the road to publishing.

Bibliography

Bettner, Betty Lou and Amy Lew. *Raising Kids Who Can.* Canada: HarperCollins, 1992.

Coloroso, Barbara. *Kids Are Worth It!* Toronto: Penguin Group, 2010.

Dreikurs, Rudolf. *Children: The Challenge.* New York: Penguin Group, 1964.

Dreikurs, Rudolf. *Social Equality: The Challenge of Today.* Chicago: Alfred Adler Institute of Chicago, 1971.

Faber, Adele and Elaine Mazlish. *How to Talk So Kids Will Listen and Listen So Kids Will Talk.* New York: Avon Books, 1980.

Faber, Adele and Elaine Mazlish. *Siblings Without Rivalry.* New York: Avon Books, 1987.

Goleman, Daniel. *Emotional Intelligence.* New York: Bantam Books, 1995.

Gordon, Thomas. *Parent Effectiveness Training.* New York: Three Rivers Press, 1970.

Kindlon, Dan and Michael Thompson. *Raising Cain.* New York: Ballantine Books, 1999.

Mozak, Harold H. *Early Recollections: Interpretive Method and Application.* New York: Routledge, 2005.

Nelsen, Jane. *Positive Discipline.* New York: Ballantine Books, 1981.

ABOUT THE AUTHORS

Doone Estey, BA, MA, is a Certified Adlerian Parent Educator along with her work for Parenting Network. She is in demand as an expert parenting speaker throughout the Greater Toronto Area, giving school courses, corporate talks, and conference keynotes. An authoritative facilitator and parenting consultant, Doone motivates parents to be their best, and her relaxed, no-nonsense style of communicating resonates immediately. Aside from being a Principal of Parenting Network, she does private parent consulting and is the Secretary-Treasurer of the Family Education Section of the North American Society of Adlerian Psychology. Doone is the mother of four children and lives with her husband in Toronto.

Beverley Cathcart-Ross founded Parenting Network in 1989. She is a leading parenting expert and international speaker, and she was recently hailed, by *Toronto Life*, as "Toronto's Top Parenting Guru." She has appeared as a guest expert on TVOntario, CBC, Breakfast Television, and CTS, and in many publications, including *Today's Parent*, *Canadian Family*, *Reader's Digest*, and *Chatelaine*. Beverley is the producer of a successful CD series that includes the sessions *Self-Esteem, What's Your Style, Who's the Boss, Keeping the Peace*, and *Setting Limits*. Beverley's natural charisma warms up a crowd and inspires hope in even the most discouraged parent. She is an active member of the North American Society of Adlerian Psychology. Beverley, a mother of four, lives in Toronto with her husband.

Martin Nash, M.D., was in family practice for nineteen years and then specialized in Psychotherapy and Family Counseling using Alfred Alder's psychology. He has run a successful practice for the past thirty years, helping transform relationships for thousands of individuals. Martin and his wife, Georgine, were instrumental in bringing parent education to Toronto. Martin has conducted presentations and training for professionals throughout North America. He has three sons and six grandchildren and lives an active life with his wife in Toronto.

ABOUT PARENTING NETWORK

Parenting Network Inc., based in Toronto, Canada, has a full range of products and services for parents. You can learn on your own from your home, join a group course, attend a teleseminar or webinar, or schedule one-on-one coaching.

All of our programs are practical and engaging and are built on the principles shared in this book.

For full details, please visit our website:
www.parentingnetwork.ca